DISCARD

An Islam of Her Own

Contents

Acknowledgments

In many ways, this book has been like Rumi's "guesthouse," a guesthouse where many visitors were welcome, some more than others, and still, I hope, many more to come. Rumi evokes the ways that books, like humans, often require an openness to the unexpected: both the joy and the sorrows that one's guesthouse of life make possible.

> This being human is a guesthouse. Every morning a new arrival. A joy, a depression, a meanness, some momentary awareness comes as an unexpected visitor. Welcome and entertain them all! Even if they're a crowd of sorrows, who violently sweep your house empty of its furniture, still, treat each guest honorably. He may be clearing you out for some new delight. . . . Be grateful for whoever comes, because each has been sent as a guide from beyond. (Rumi's *Masnavi*)

One important visitor without whom this book would not have been possible is my mentor and adviser, Suad Joseph, who inspired and guided me throughout the long and lonely research and writing process of the last eight years. Her keen perception and advice opened many windows in my guesthouse. I am deeply indebted to her for her support and the unlimited energy and time she dedicated to me and to this project. It goes without saying, however, that any omissions, errors, or limitations in this text are mine alone.

I also am very grateful for having had an exceptional doctoral committee and wish to thank Ira Lapidus, Juana Rodriguez, and Omnia El Shakry. I am especially thankful to Omnia El Shakry's enthusiasm, her positive encouragement to "get this book out!" and for her insistence on always putting reality to the test of history.

My deep thanks to Katherine Pratt Ewing for her interest in my work. She shared many of her insights with me, and her work on multiplicity in subjectivity inspired me. My thanks as well to my friends and colleagues from various universities, who read either parts or whole versions of this book and gave me valuable insights and encouragement: Barbara Aswad, Lara Deeb, and Susan Slymovicks; and, from UC Riverside, Carol Tushabe, Vivian Nyitray, Jonathan Walton, Sherri Johnson, Feryal Cherif, Christine Gailey, and Tom Patterson. My sincere thanks to Jennifer Hammer, my editor at NYU Press for her unfailing energy, experience, and superb editorial talents, which were the dynamo behind this book's publication. Finally, my acknowledgments would not be complete without a heartfelt thanks to the generous visitors who remained, often for longest stretches of time in my guesthouse, the Islamic activist women of al-Hilal in Cairo, who shared their lives, dreams, and hopes with me. I am indebted to them for their generosity.

I cannot describe how grateful I am to my mother and father for their support and love. I went through the experience of losing my father in the process of finishing this book. His loss urged me to get the manuscript through the finishing line as a way of thanking him for being such an amazing human being. My father first opened my eyes to the excitement of reading and the possibilities of unlearning. It is to him that I dedicate this book. My mother has been an unfailing pillar of strength and support for me, despite how challenging I often made it for her. Her steadfast love and support continue to inspire me. Mother, I could not have come this far without you.

Of everyone mentioned here, no one has been as impacted by the process of writing this book as my children, Ziad el-Gamal and Hana el-Gamal. They have my deepest gratitude. Their patience and unwavering belief in me were the most welcome in my guesthouse. I cannot express here how touching their support has been throughout this time. They were my companions and cheerleaders in California, where I completed my doctorate, and in Cairo, while I spent countless hours finishing this book, and back again in California. They never once complained nor wavered in their support of my efforts. I love you both.

The continuous love, support, and humor of my partner, Joe Brooks, were instrumental to the completion of this book. He is surely what Rumi meant by "a new delight." He sustained me when I was at the end of my tether, cooking my meals and brewing me coffee and tea to keep me awake at night when I needed to meet my deadlines. He had the patience to read through the whole book more than once. For all this and much more, I recognize the wonderful gift that he is to me.

Finally, my acknowledgments end with the hope that this book welcomes all visitors and guests.

1

Introducing Desiring Subjects

Climbing up the stairs to the main hall of the building of al-Hilal, an Islamic private voluntary organization (PVO) nestled in the suburbs of Cairo,[1] I was met by the reading class's familiar rhythmic recital of the Qur'an.[2] Filtering through the animated hum of conversation and the chimes of cell phones ringing from the far corners of the hall, voices rose and fell in perfect unison. The smell of baking wafted through the kitchen door, calling attention to the culinary skills of the cooking team who were preparing their baked goods for sale. Wrapped in cellophane, freshly baked *konafa* and *baqlawa* were carried out by a number of unresisting visitors who walked past me as I stepped inside.

Dalia, an activist at the *gam'iyah*,[3] was waiting for me in her workshop where she trained women to produce and market crafts as part of the center's vocational program. After offering me a cool Pepsi on that hot summer day, Dalia leaned against one of the long tables in the room as she casually chatted about her children. Her oldest son, now seventeen, was graduating from high school that year. "I worry about young people today," she said. "The school system is in shambles. Parents who have schoolchildren don't have a clue to what to expect next from the ministry (of education). Throwing her arms into the air, Dalia exclaimed exasperatedly, "The system of education needs to change." I agreed, and our conversation veered to my own research.

Dalia and I had briefly discussed my work before, but she asked again why I was focusing on al-Hilal's activism. I explained that I had become interested in women and Islamic activism when I read about Heba Raouf, who is a leading scholar on Islam in the Middle East and a professor of political science at Cairo University.[4] Dalia seemed interested, though perplexed. Perhaps she needed reassurance that I would find al-Hilal's activism interesting for the right reasons,[5]—and perhaps this is what prompted her to jump up suddenly and beckon me to follow, suggesting, "Why don't you talk to Doctora Zeinab about all this? Come, come, she will be very interested."

I hesitated, wondering whether Doctora Zeinab (*doctora* means doctor; Doctora Zeinab was a physician) would really be interested in my work. After all, I was there to learn about them, not the other way around, or so I thought, not realizing that only a few minutes later, these roles of researcher and researched would be completely reversed. In any case, I had no choice but to follow Dalia out the door and into the small crowded office of Doctora Zeinab, the director of the PVO. The researcher was becoming the researched, I thought to myself.[6] Doctora Zeinab sat behind her desk facing the doorway, surrounded by a group of women activists.

My mind raced back to my first meeting with the *doctora*. At the time, I was working on a book on the notion of empowerment in feminist literature dealing with "Islamic women activists" (Hafez 2003). Laila, a friend of mine, had introduced me to *gam'iyat* al-Hilal and, after some initial reluctance, took me to meet Doctora Zeinab. Laila's hesitation was due to the fact that the media had been leading a bitter campaign against the emergence of *da'iyat*, or "women preachers,"[7] ridiculing women's turn to Islam. Newspaper and magazine articles painted a portrait of *da'iyat* as naïve and misled, accusing them of being mouthpieces for conservative Islamist groups.

Doctora Zeinab looked up at me as Dalia recounted our earlier conversation to her. I was once again struck by the strength of her presence and her reflective gaze that seemed to miss nothing. When Doctora Zeinab spoke, she had a deep resonating voice that in its clearly enunciated Arabic claimed attention. Articulate with her words, strong in asserting her thoughts, she exuded an air of confidence and self-assurance that was as unassuming as it was impressive. These recollections sped through my mind as I, once again, received her steady gaze. The group of women in the room shifted their attention to our presence. Like Doctora Zeinab, some were dressed in long-sleeved blouses and a long skirt that reached below the ankles, whereas others wore long dresses. Most of the activists at the *gam'iyah* wore a *hijab*, or headscarf that covered their hair and neck. The variety in the colors and designs of the *hijab*s added interest to the otherwise austere surroundings.

Dalia finished introducing me, explaining that I was back to do more work on Islamic activism at al-Hilal. "*Kheir* . . . [good]," Doctora Zeinab responded, "the more interest there is in our work, the more awareness of those in need of help in society will grow." "This is *kheir*," she repeated while seeming to be contemplating something in the distance. There was silence as she looked around the room. Then Doctora Zeinab turned to me once again and pointedly asked, "Why do you do what you do?" Aware that something important hinged on my response, I paused, sensing all eyes upon me, and wondered in that split second about that myself. I realized that it was the thrill of unlearning that drives me "to do what I do" and the possibilities of other ways of knowing that brought me here. This prompted me to elaborate on my research and to describe my commitment to understanding al-Hilal's kind of activism. Doctora Zeinab nodded her understanding and then in her deep voice addressed everyone in the room, "Kol wahid fina 'ando hadaf [Each of us has a goal]. Wi kol wahid fina biyhaqaq al-hadaf dah bi tariqtoh [And each one of us pursues this goal in his or her own way]." She smiled this time as she looked at me, and her face lit up. My journey, though seeking a different destination, was hers, too.

After these few minutes of conversation, I realized with a start that I was now sitting at Doctora Zeinab's desk, that at some point someone must have offered me her chair in front of the desk, and that I must have sat down on it. The women in the room were now standing around us in a semicircle; they, too, were part of this exchange. It was then that it dawned on me that something in the room had shifted. A palpable bond was established during that brief exchange. During my conversation with her, Doctora Zeinab managed to bring us all together. A new energy encircled us, and this time I was a part of it. I was not merely an observer or simply a researcher, but like the activist women of the *gam'iyah* who stood with me in that small office, I was a desiring subject.

Subject Production and the Heterogeneity of Desire

The women of the organization of al-Hilal and I, shaped by an array of impulses and yearnings that drive the unstable production of postmodern subjecthood, shared desire as a productive force that makes possible who we are. Desire both creates and, in turn, is created by cultural and social experiences, by historical traditions, by state agendas, and by individual negotiations. In the moment just described at al-Hilal, the acknowledgment of desire for one's own passions, goals, and needs seemed to speak to all of us in the room, however diverse our ultimate aims may have been.

Desire, a process that is always incomplete, fragmented, often contradictory, and unstable, explodes the analysis of subjectivity beyond the notion of the unitary individual assumed in modern liberal discourse. A focus on the production of desire as embedded in wider imbrications of colonialism, nationalism, and projects of modernization, secularization, and Islamization captures the complex range of subject positions among desiring subjects in women's Islamic movements today.

An Islam of Her Own examines the desires and subjecthood of activist Islamic women by exploring the inseparability of piety and the political project. It is concerned with destabilization, inconsistency, and impermanence in subject production, identity formation, and cultural transformation in Islamic movements. Its objective is to enable an understanding of the heterogeneity of desire and subjectivity that embedded discourses of religion and secularism make possible, in scholarship on Islamic movements, transnational feminism, religion, and religious activism.

In considering the mutual embeddedness of religion and secularism, *An Islam of Her Own* builds on a body of literature that has continued to work on describing—albeit in different ways—this vexed relationship, which often takes the seemingly normative shape of polemics between secular modernity and Islam (Asad 2003; Deeb 2006; Mahmood 2005; Özyürek 2006). I extend the questions raised in this literature by asking how a theoretical concomitance of religion and secularism as mutually productive discourses can open new considerations of desire and subject production in Islamic movements. In so doing, my intent is to further the discussion of the mutuality of religion and secularism in the modern Middle East by foregrounding the heterogeneity of desire in my analysis of subjecthood. I ask the following questions: What are the processes that shape, shift, incite, and produce the desires and subjectivities of women in Islamic movements? How do women activists articulate their desires, and how do these desires mirror the complexity of negotiation, inculcation, and inconsistent appropriation and individual experience?

I argue that the desires of women activists in Islamic movements in Egypt today cannot be fully grasped through a focus on unitary ethical subjects based only on religious practice. Instead, I contend that subjecthood is varied, heterogeneous, and unstable. Subject making cannot be understood as a continuous process within a single paradigm. Whether inculcated through social and cultural processes or cultivated through self-directed and embodied practices, subject making should be considered as deeply embedded in wider, complex, and imbricated social and historical processes. As my point of departure, I take the situatedness of subjectivity and desire in the complex debates of Islamic practice, modernity, postcoloniality, and nation-state building processes in Egypt. My approach relies on an understanding of "desire" as the multifarious wants and needs that underlie subject formation. I understand desire to be an ongoing process rather than an ultimate objective. In this, I follow Gilles Deleuze and Félix Guattari's (2004) notion that desire enables productive social change and, in so doing, undermines systems of power. This understanding enables the analysis to take account of subjectivity as a perpetual state of becoming. I adopt the metaphor of the "rhizome" in this book to describe heterogeneous and multifaceted desires. *Rhizome* is a term for directions in motion that are not necessarily linear (Deleuze and Guattari 1983). Because the rhizome has no center and no end, it can represent the desires of postmodern subjecthood, which defies boundedness, unity, and continuity.

My findings are based on six years of ethnographic research and observation of women's Islamic activism in Egypt between 2000 and 2003 and between 2005 and 2008, which suggest that Islamic women activists are complex, multifaceted subjects whose desires take shape through imbricated notions of pious self-amelioration and secular political values. (My use of the term *imbricated* does not mean that Islamic discourse and secularism were at some point separate and have become imbricated. In fact, I begin with the assumption that religion and secularism are seldom distinct or separate.)

In my conversations with the activist women of al-Hilal, I became aware of how they privatized their views of Islamic faith and practice. To them, religion was defined as a personal relationship with God. Politics was understood to be beyond their realm. Clearly, they desired an Islamized Egypt, yet they saw the means to achieving that goal to lie within themselves. They thus used their own understanding of Islamic teaching and practice to determine how they conducted themselves in their communities, raised their children, related to their families, and implemented sustainable projects for the underprivileged. Desires informed by mutually productive discourses of secularism and religious ideology drove their Islamic social reform projects and their vision of an Islamized society. Despite their agendas for social change, al-Hilal's activists did not view their activism as political or challenging to the hegemony of the state. Although they discursively expressed views that assumed a separation between the religious and the political, in practice their activism did not reflect these distinctions.

As desiring subjects, the activist women of al-Hilal that I came to know mirrored the projects of modernizing liberal secularism, nationalism, state-building agendas, and Islamic discourses in their own understanding of themselves and the world around them. Their narratives described personal pious journeys to self-realization. Listening to these narratives, I could not help but be struck by how unilineal and well rehearsed they sounded and, more specifically, how these stories harked back to the modern national discourses common in episodes broadcast by Egyptian television.

Lila Abu-Lughod calls these highly popular melodramas "dramas of nationhood" (2004). She argues that these television series foster a modern sense of self-awareness and interiority that emphasizes individuality in the general population of Egyptian viewers. Although they were originally conceptualized as encouraging secular modern thought, Abu-Lughod believes that television pedagogies of modern selfhood often feed into the modern identity politics of Islamism. Islamic activist women are grounded in these sociopolitical processes, and they are influenced by the media, globalization, and world events. They are living, breathing human subjects who are unbounded, temporal, and desirous and thus defy notions of unitary, fixed essences.

Centering on the narratives of stories to explore the desires that drive Islamic women activists, *An Islam of Her Own* examines the assumption that subjectivities are uniform entities consistently and separately formed apart from the constituting discourse of history. This book focuses specifically on the processes of modernization and postcolonial nation-state building to expound on the embedded, fragmented, and contradictory subject positions that individuals assume in particular historical moments and contexts.

Subjects of Islam and/or Feminism

The women of the al-Hilal private voluntary organization belong to a multifaceted movement of Islamic activism in Cairo.[8] Their version of Islamic activism reflects an array of social reform projects ranging from sustainable ventures to erase poverty to pursuing the Islamic transformation of Egyptian society. They teach literacy classes, provide health and vocational services, deliver public sermons, and widely disseminate Islamic teachings and ethics among women and children in urban and rural centers. For the first time in Egypt's history, women from various socioeconomic classes are working together on social reform movements on such a wide scale. Remarkable yet obscure initiatives have set into motion a social, political, and economic dynamic that has propelled these Islamic activists into the Egyptian public space where Islamists and secularists alike vie for control.

Since their appearance as interspersed groups in the early 1990s, women's Islamic movements in Muslim societies around the world have occupied a rather ambiguous space in the feminist literature about women in the Middle East.[9] Scholars have debated the extent to which women's Islamic activism can improve their status in society; that is, whether "Islam"—as a religious ideology—can empower women. A paradigmatic divide separates two major strands that have grappled with this issue. The first strand argues that an Islamic emancipation of women is possible (Badran 1996; Cooke 2001; Fernea 1998), whereas the second is suspicious of an agenda for emancipation couched in religious terms (Moghissi 1999; Mojab 2001; Shahidian 2002).

The debate soon came to revolve around whether or not activist Islamic women could be considered feminist. Haideh Moghissi (1999, 146) posed the question that epitomized this development: "Is Islamic feminism a brand of feminism or a brand of Islamism?" To Moghissi, an Islamic feminism can be only an arm of Islamic fundamentalism and thus impedes, not enables, liberation. She reasons that women who participate in Islamic movements are the misled victims of a religious ideology. The underlying belief here is that religion—and particularly fundamentalist religion—is, by its very nature, oppressive. According to Moghissi, one therefore cannot be both feminist and religious. Deniz Kandiyoti (1996), discusses the futility of theory that attempts to join feminism to Islam. She contends that since feminism and Islam emerge from distinct historical and ideological trajectories, they cannot simply be rationalized as one phenomenon.

In sum, the approaches employed to discern the liberatory potential of women's Islamic movements have tended to rely primarily on normative assumptions that binarize religion and secularism. Consequently, women who subscribe to an Islamic agenda are viewed either as pious subjects who belong to a traditional ideology that denies them the rationality and freedom accorded to modern secular subjects or as feminist subjects whose empowerment is contingent on their success in adapting their religious agenda to a liberal secularist one. The absence of a clear problematization of the imbricated relationship between Islamism and secularism obscures women's desires in Islamic movements. The location of these activists in the matrices of power in postcolonialist processes of nation-building, modernization,[10] and secularization projects[11] represents individuals engaged in religious movements as unitary ethical subjects. They are either resistant or oppressed, feminist or not, modern or traditional. Exceptions to these approaches include Minoo Moallem (1999), who offers a nonbinary approach; Salwa Ismail (2006), who places the largest emphasis on the need to historically, socioeconomically, and spatially contextualize Islamic activism; and Carolyn Rouse (2004), who offers an example of a well-contextualized approach to studying subjectivity in conversions to Islam in the United States.[12]

Because I view desire as heterogeneous and inconsistent, I acknowledge in this book the complexity of women's subjectivities in their engagement with Islamic movements. Rather than beginning by ascribing a "religious" or "secular" nature to these desires, let us consider how processes of subjectification are always negotiated and incomplete. My analysis situates the discussion of subject production in religious movements—in our case, Islamic movements—within concomitant, embedded, and imbricated notions of secularism and religion.

What would these subjectivities look like if we dispensed with the dichotomous analytical categories of "Islam" and "secularism"? How would we articulate the desires underlying subjecthood that are part of Islamic movements in Muslim societies today? To overcome the binary between Islam and modernity that persists in discourse—both in the media and among Islamists and state political mouthpieces—Lara Deeb (2006), an anthropologist of Islam and modernities, proposed the idea of "the enchanted modern" as a useful theoretical idiom. Debunking these dichotomous views at the level of subjectivity, Deeb offers the "enchanted modern" as a metaphor for the pious Shi'i Lebanese, who are capable of grappling with the complexities of modern life by merging piety and "modern-ness." This term is helpful in breaking down the binary assumption of an "antimodern" Islam and a "modern" West. But how can we explain the slippages, inconsistencies, and conjunctures in subject formation that the complex histories of colonialism, modernity, Islamization and state formation make possible?

In this book, I problematize the yearnings, wants, and "desires" of subjects engaged in Islamic movements as multifarious heterogeneous and discontinuous processes of subjectivity. My intent is to take the discussion of desire beyond dualities, to allow desires to speak through their subjects and not through the analytical categories that I apply to them. My aim is to understand desire as a multifaceted process that is not continuous or uniform and to stress the moments of slippage and disruption that mirror the individual imbrications, daily negotiations, and unpredictable concomitance of religion and liberal secularity. I want to probe the processes that, to Gayatri Spivak, "exceeded the borders of the intending subject" (2005, 481). In pursuing these processes of inculcation, I focus on the contextual and mutual imbrications of the constructs of "religion" and "modernity." These imbrications are the means by which individuals negotiate modern life and cultivate modes of discipline. They also are processes grounded in desires inculcated in subjecthood through wider sociopolitical and historical discourses.

Anthropologist Saba Mahmood significantly influenced the field of gender in the Middle East with her argument for a nonliberal model of agency. Mahmood presents the desires of women in Egypt's "mosque movement" as "nonliberal" models of agency demonstrating that liberal feminism "sharply limits our ability to understand and interrogate the lives of women whose *desire, affect, and will have been shaped by non-liberal traditions*"(2001, 203, italics added). In her critique of the normative liberal definition of agency contingent on forms of resistance, she shows that women participants in this mosque movement are agentive through their bodily inculcation of piety and religious discipline and thereby produce a different kind of politics. To Mahmood, *veiling* is a "selving" technique in which individuals cultivate certain qualities of the self. As a selving technique, veiling gives the body humility and modesty. These "nonliberal" inculcations, Mahmood argues, challenge dominant secular liberal feminist frameworks of agency that adopt resistance and freedom as their preconditions. Instead, these women's agency is predicated on submission to religious practices that, when repeatedly performed, discipline their bodies and allow for a situational and historically specific agency (Mahmood 2005).

I draw on Mahmood's intervention to explore desire and subject production in postcolonialist societies that have experienced the complicated processes of nation building, sociopolitical projects of modernization, and Islamization. Instead of accepting the notion of a fixed essence of what is liberal or nonliberal[13] in Islamic practices—(I agree with Mahmood that the attempt to redeem lost elements is often futile)—the task most salient to analyzing the desires that animate these movements is to ask, as James Clifford did, "What processes rather than essences are involved in present experiences of cultural identity?" (1988, 275).

Mahmood maintains that most of the participants in the piety movement believe that veiling is a necessary component of modesty. She emphasizes that for her informants, veiling is not an outward expression of interiority but a disciplinary process that instills modesty. In other words, the veil is not an outward expression of interior feelings of modesty but a means of cultivating modesty. While I agree with Mahmood that these reversals in exteriority/interiority contest normative liberal understandings of resistance, I still wonder how pious women's desire for veiling is shaped. How can we understand their choice to produce the "kind of subject presumed to be necessary to the political imaginary of the piety movement"? (Mahmood 2005, 152). How is desire produced for this kind of subjecthood so central to the piety movement that Mahmood studied? To the participants of this pious movement, the qualities that women seek to cultivate and the kinds of subjects that they aspire to be cannot be imagined outside the wider context of sociocultural processes. Therefore, without understanding these larger contexts, we cannot fully glean the parameters of subject formation among the movement's participants.

For example, veiling has long been a central issue brought about by conflicting histories of Qur'anic interpretation, colonialism, resistance, and Islamization (Ahmed 1992; Hoodfar 2001; Mernissi 1991). By constructing practices of veiling and segregation of women in Muslim societies as socially backward and unjust customs, colonialist discourse sought to undermine patriarchal structures by challenging local masculinities (Lazreg 1994). Conversely, modernizing elites of newly emerging nation-states, seeking to reconfigure social structures and gender roles, also emphasized issues of segregation and veiling practices as backward and not modern. Islamist responses to Western centric notions of progress often use the veil as a marker of the Islamization of the public sphere, whereas current feminist narratives by Muslim women in Western societies see the veil as an assertion of their public autonomy.

Taking account of these discursive processes of veiling is necessary to understanding the cultivation of ideals of comportment and ethical virtues of modesty among pious subjects. Although scholars have argued that veiling is a pre-Islamic tradition (e.g., Ahmed 1992, Mernissi 1991), wearing a veil is perceived today as an act of Islamic piety. When Muslim women "cultivate" piety by wearing a headscarf, they are simultaneously inculcated by discourses of colonialism, nationalism, liberal modernity, and local and global politics, in which both liberal and nonliberal imbrications configure their choices and practices and even their articulations of piety and ethical forms.

In this book, I move my analysis from Mahmood's insightful work on nonliberal agency to call into question the consistency of nonliberal agency. Given the complex and mutually imbricated discursive history of Islam and secularism in the Egyptian context, the subjectivities and desires of women in Islamic movements cannot be captured fully as a nonliberal model in which a consistent religious subject is set on a coherent path to self-transformation. Where do the inconsistencies, disruptions, and multiplicities in the subject positions of women participants in Islamic movements find a place in this analysis? Rather than claim a priori that the research begins with nonliberal subjects, I follow Michel Foucault (1979) in arguing that subject positions are discursively produced.

Desiring modern subjects lie at the nexus of ambivalence, contradiction, and heterogeneity in discourses of modernity. Consequently, subjecthood can never be truly captured as a single subject position in which the self[14] undergoes a consistent and uniform journey of self-fashioning. Desire is an important point of departure for capturing subjectivity in its intensity and acts as the driving force creating the impetus for its very being.[15]

Anthropologist Suad Joseph's 2005 investigation of the desiring female subject and relational pedagogies still remains the only theoretical contribution to studies of desire in the Middle East. Joseph's ethnographic study, set in Lebanon, relates desire to notions of selfhood. She challenges the Western feminist premise that views desire only in relation to bounded individuals and contends that desire is relationally produced. Hence, Joseph determines that desire may be understood in terms not limited to a liberal notion of selfhood. Instead, her conception of desire allows for a nuanced understanding of these experiencing subjects, who inhabit multiple spaces and engage in Islamic activism that reflects the mutual embeddedness of religion and secularism. The activist women of al-Hilal epitomize these heterogeneous desires, which can only be described as unbounded. To me, they also represent various dimensions of a dilemma.

In an earlier work (2003), I addressed the role of Islamic activism in empowering women in Egypt and concluded that the empowerment I saw was perceived through a limiting lens and couched in terms that were antithetical to liberal models of development literature. Through a pedagogical inquiry into religious practice, mastery of the tenets of Islamic jurisprudence (*sunnah*),[16] and social activism, women activists pursued a Muslim ideal of womanhood. Yet I noted that in their actions, words, ideals, practices, and goals that they often did not follow an entirely Islamic historical trajectory. It became evident to me that I was not dealing with bounded Islamic subjectivities that were consistently redefining and distilling their image of a pure "Islam." While the women of al-Hilal asserted their bond with a single religious paradigm, they described their pursuit of *al-taqarub lilah* (getting closer to God) and the positioning of Islamic teaching as guiding principles for everything they did. The same women made normalized distinctions between religion and secularism that were liberal in principle and secular in practice while simultaneously viewing Islam as encompassing all aspects of life. Why did these moments of slippage occur? What do they indicate, and how can they inform our understanding of desire and subject making among Islamic activists like the women of al-Hilal? These moments of slippage reaffirm the argument made in this book, suggesting that subjecthood is varied, heterogeneous, and unstable.

Next I show how historical processes of colonialism, nationalism, and modernization hone subjects in deep, visceral ways. I explore how postcolonial desire molds subjectivity and seek to produce modern, obedient subjects of the state. Processes of modernity, postcoloniality, nation-state building in Egypt, and an engagement with Islam provide the impetus for subject making among Islamic activisits. Desire is at the center of these processes, which simultaneously inculcate and cultivate modern liberal values. But desires are not consistently formed, nor are they homogenous and uniform across populations. Moreover, desiring subjects often resist inculcation and cultivate by means of selving techniques those qualities that contradict hegemonic processes of subject production.

Postcolonial Desire and Subjectivity

My main concern in this book is to describe the geographies of desire that underlie subject formation in women's Islamic activism in Egypt. Having underscored the fluidity and heterogeneity of desire in modern subjecthood and the plurality of spheres that engender these desires, I turn next to the diverse ways in which postcoloniality is mapped onto these geographies of desire. Here I use the term *postcolonial* to refer to the commingled processes of state and nation building, modernization programs, and legacies of colonialism.

Although Michel Foucault (1979) brilliantly explained how the subject is discursively produced in shifting relations of power, he did not specifically address the phenomenon of colonialism. His work linking power to knowledge, however, has had a great impact on the study of the disciplinary systems of modern life in postcolonialist studies. Foucault moves our normative understanding of power as located in the state's legal and judicial apparatus to discourse as the means through which power operates.

Then, in his seminal work on the imperialist production of knowledge in the Middle East and Islamic societies, Edward Said applied Foucault's theories of power to his concept of Orientalism (1978). Here, the term *Orientalism* refers to the discursive body of knowledge produced in the nineteenth century by learned scholars, travel writers, poets, and novelists who made the Orient a repository of Western knowledge rather than societies and cultures functioning in their own spatial and temporal terms. According to Said, the Orient was created as *the inferior other* of the West, thus enabling the conceptual creation of a civilized and superior imperialist hegemonic power like the British Empire. These discursive formations were historically produced and imbued with a truth that rendered them unquestionable. Said argued that the production of text during that time period was what made these discourses "real."

Of central importance in Said's argument is how these forms of knowledge were able to indoctrinate populations with desires that produced specific articulations of personhood that responded more readily to Western domination and the consumption of Western ideas and products. The emphasis on liberal qualities of autonomy, individuality, boundedness, and rationality in these discursive processes of desire making were not, however, uniformly internalized and were not simply imprinted onto colonized subjects. Instead, these desires for modern liberal selfhood were entangled with, and mutually dependent on, local forms of comportment and subjectivity.

Dipesh Chakrabarty (1992) argued that in India, colonial modernity and nationalist thought led to the notion of "becoming individual," indicating the state of becoming an autonomous, self-regulating subject of liberal individualism. This notion of individuality assumed the dimensions of a universal human project predicated on the construct of modern citizenship. Colonialist and nationalist programs that sought the application of European liberal modern reforms did not implement them in a vacuum; rather, these reforms merged—sometimes uncomfortably—with alternative ways of thinking about the self and society. According to Chakrabarty, "these themes have existed—

in contestation, alliance, and miscegenation—with other narratives of the self and community that do not look to the state/citizen bind as the ultimate construct of sociality" (1992, 10). Despite the differences between British colonialism in India and its administration of Egypt, and the nationalist government agendas of each, Chakrabarty's contention places importance on considering the ways in which discourses of modernity exist in multiple forms of subject formation.

Liberal modernist discourses continue to make normative the distinctions between secularism and religion. Secularism persists as the defining factor of modernization, together with the assumption that the further religion enters the public sphere, the less modernization propagates. It is not a coincidence that global warfare around the world is still, in the second millennium, predominantly shaped as an ideological confrontation between the tenets of democratic life and the "backward fanaticism" of religious groups. In order for secularism to dominate the public sphere, a number of modernizing states in the Middle East set in motion institutional shifts to structure a new discursive space in which religion could exist without impinging on public life. In postcolonial Egypt, Talal Asad (2003) points out, that to minimize Islam's presence in the public sphere, a new space had to be created for it. This new space, he contended, was the construction of the private realm of the modern Egyptian family, in which the Islamic *shari'a*, as the new form of privatized religion, was to govern family relations and help construct self-governing subjects.

The project of secularizing public space does not end with limiting religion, as it also allows a reorganization of social practices. In colonial and national governance, constructs of "private" and "public" are conceptual tools for ordering society. Separating the domestic realm from that of the state is one of the powerful ways by which the latter can control the personal and the social. The creation of a public sphere of politics, as opposed to the private domain of the religious, enables modern forms of secular governance. These spaces are often gendered, with the public enforcing a masculine character and the private becoming the location of the feminine. Despite these distinctive binaries, modern state administrations regulate the domestic domain by emphasizing education and schooling as a strategy for creating the secular government's new bodies, subjectivities, and citizens and testifying to the porous nature of these demarcations in material terms while emphasizing their demarcations in ideological constructs.

To this end, Tim Mitchell (1991) cautioned against the normalization of the boundaries between the state and society and called for an understanding of states as "an effect" rather than a separate entity. Considering the fluidity of the state and society allows for a more critical view of the ways that social processes reproduce themselves in the context of state hegemony. Disciplinary power does not exist merely as an external imposition on the individual but also emerges from within: "Disciplines work from within local domains and institutions, entering into particular social processes, breaking them down into separate functions, rearranging the parts, increasing their efficiency and precision, and reassembling them into more productive and powerful combinations" (Mitchell 1991, 18). More important, Mitchell departs from this Foucauldian premise to assert that disciplinary methods are neither consistent nor always coherent. They may also be contradictory and are not immune to breakdown.

Awareness of the lack of homogeneity of disciplinary power helps us avoid overestimating the state's role in producing normative homogenous subjects of power. In addition, this perspective allows for a consideration of the creative ways in which individuals maneuver their own space to counter the state's hegemony over its disciplinary institutions. Individuals often use the state institutions' disciplinary methods in their own organizational techniques. For instance, in their sustainable development project in the village of Mehmeit, I noted that the activist women of al-Hilal applied behaviors, teachings, and strategies similar to those in the state's modernization schemes.

The intersections of historical, material, and ideological forces create the impetus for desire in postcolonial subjects. Suffused with ambivalence, contestation, and fragmentation, desire is shaped by incomplete, contradictory, and unpredictable fields of power relations. The desires of activist women who participate in the Islamic movement in Egypt are similarly shaped by such dynamics. Their desires map out new geographies as they negotiate emerging entanglements and rework crucial sites of power in both their communities and themselves. An example is the Islamic activism that propels the women of al-Hilal into new social arenas. I observed this in the village of Mehmeit where two activist women began the social development of the small community there. Even though they initially were met with indifference by the village women, the Islamic activists gradually assumed positions of respect and high regard. Liberal modern desires merged with Islamic agendas as the activist women continued to work in the village. In such instances, we can view the productive potential of historical imbrications to incite change. Desires for Islamic social reform, fluid and imbricated with postcolonialist histories and ideologies, incited change at both the material level, in the village's living conditions, and the discursive level, at which issues of gender, class, education, and religion restructured the villagers' views.

Desires shaped by the temporal dynamics of colonialism, modernization, secularization, and nation-building projects present complex and heterogeneous forms of subjectivity. Persistent theoretical models of religious selves engaged in continuous self-fashioning toward a fixed "religious ideal" ignore the complexity and seamlessness of the desires animating these subjectivities. Moreover, secularist principles and Islamic practices are not binaries, as they are constructed in the state's liberal modern discourse. Indeed, they are mutually embedded in the practices and behaviors of the women with whom I worked at al-Hilal. Whereas Islamic principles guided the projects of social development at al-Hilal, the activists' goals, desires, and subjecthood were imbricated with secular liberal norms of nationhood and postcoloniality.

Women participants who engage in Islamic movements today often proclaim in their narratives a departure from their past secular selves as a marker of becoming Islamically pious. They often attribute to themselves a bounded religious nature while also expressing desires and motivations that reflect a secular character. Katherine Ewing (1990) called this tendency to subsume fragmentation an "illusion of wholeness," in which people experience themselves as a timeless "whole" in a particular context. She quotes the work of Fernandez (1986), who studied the use by participants in religious movements of religious imagery that was often inconsistent, carefully chosen, and ordered into a "timeless whole." In Ewing's view, people construct themselves through carefully chosen cultural concepts of personhood and selected "chains" of personal memories.

In a later work, Ewing (1997) rejected the premise that hegemonic discourses are often naturalized uncritically and embedded in individual consciousness. She explained that experiencing subjects are not the unitary, willing recipients of constitutive discourses:

> Discourses constitute subject positions, but the experiencing subject is a non unitary agent (perhaps better described as a bundle of agencies) who—in part through the experience of competing ideologies and alternative discourses—operates with a potential for critical distance from one discourse or subject position, including a discourse of modernity. (1997, 5)

Ewing advocates a "theoretical space for a *desiring experiencing subjectivity that stands at the nexus of discourse*. It is this space which enables a critically conscious center of experience" (1997, 5, italics added).

In his study of narratives of self-construction, Wolfgang Krauss (2000) asserts that this genre of dialogic selfhood is fundamentally modern. In the narratives he examines, the liberal enterprising individual creates identities that mark transitions in modern configurations in a constantly changing social context. He quotes Peter Wagner: "These transitions entail social processes of disembedding and provoke transformations of social identities, in the course of which not only other identities are acquired but the possibility of construction is also widely perceived" (1994, 157). These processes of "disembedding" that Wagner mentions can be considered as the means by which participants select what they deem an Islamic ideal and disembed what is perceived as extraneous to their principles of self-transformations.

Knowledge lies at the heart of these self-making processes. "I will never forget these days," Mona Yunis, an Islamic activist, recounted in her novel *Wagh bala makyadj* (*A Face without Makeup*), "when we learned verses of the Koran by heart and read Koranic interpretations and other useful books. In that way I learned the importance of knowledge in our life, and that ignorance stresses notions of completeness, coherence, and sequential stages of self-realization." Thus Islamic women activists construct new selves in contrast to their past ones. "Ignorance is the tragedy of Muslims. I am sorry to say it, but they are ignorant concerning both religious knowledge and secular knowledge. Actually, the first step to obedience to God is knowledge and education. God will pave the way to paradise for the one who takes the path of knowledge" (1993, 94). Yunis emphasizes knowledge and education as forms of self-fashioning. To her, ignorance is an impediment to being pious, and educated pious individuals will be rewarded by God. Here, education is a basis for Islamic piety while simultaneously acting as a central trope of the state's modernizing discourse in Egypt.

In their modern narratives, where they juxtapose their secular selves with their Islamic subjectivities, Islamic activist women seek to constitute their identities and validate their claims for a new Islamic direction. Are these two selves really as demarcated and separate as their narratives make them out to be? I think not. Rather than focusing on collective stories about arrivals, I look at the act of journeying itself. This is where I was privileged to share the processes of subject production by women activists. A complex and intertwined construction of Islamic personhood is inculcated at the same time as it is cultivated. While our Islamic activist women of al-Hilal purposefully cultivate new Muslim subjectivities, they are informed not only by their own personal understanding of Islamic practices and ideals but also by their choices, selections, and emphasis on these teachings, drawing on internalized modern assumptions that histories of modernizing state agendas have rendered normative in their populations. Yet, as Ewing (1997) reminds us, individuals possess multiple agencies and are willing and capable of assuming critical distance from discourses of modernity. This book pays particular attention to these discontinuities, the abrupt halts, and rebeginnings that women who participate in Islamic movements experience. Through these moments of disjuncture, I was able to trace the possibilities in women's desires that enable their Islamic activism in Egypt and to understand the ways by which women define religion, understand political action, and envision social change.

Journeys of Becoming and Transformation: Women's Subjecthood in Islamic Activism

This book looks at how women who participate in Islamic activism narrate their selfhood, articulate their desires, and embody discourses that blur the boundaries between the religious and the secular. By tracing the concomitance between the complex debates of modernity and postcoloniality and the various heterogeneous and contradictory subject positions that individuals inhabit in particular historical moments and contexts, I try to unsettle the assumptions that subjectivities are uniform entities formed through ahistorical constitutive discourses. I cannot, however, ignore the subject's lived and complex experience in multiple discourses and material conditions, given that all knowledge is necessarily incomplete and partial. Rosi Braidotti (1994) emphasized the importance of developing new kinds of feminist figurations. For her, as well as for the approach I take in this book, postmodern deconstructions and critiques are politically empowering and open new possibilities when sustained by a critical consciousness.

In a sprawling metropolis like Cairo, which is the largest Islamic city in the world and also the leading urban center for Islamic movements, it is possible to travel without crossing a border. Cairo is the ideal location for studying women's Islamic activism. Although officially secular, Egypt's personal status laws (*qanun al ahwal al shakhsia*), which are based on *shari'a*,[17] regulate family life, marriage, divorce, and especially women's position in society. While predominantly Muslim, Egypt is not, however, an Islamic state. Women's activism often escapes direct state policing. Aside from complying with the regulations of the Ministry of Social Affairs (MOSA), Islamic women activists in Egypt operate a number of private voluntary organizations somewhat independently from the state, although on rare occasions they become the object of sporadic but intense scrutiny.[18] Whereas men's Islamic groups are banned from political participation, women's Islamic social activism enjoys a certain measure of autonomy. For example, women's activities tend to be scrutinized less closely than men's are. Women activists raise funds and work anywhere they please, and the state does not generally hinder their mobility. Even though it is obscured by their lack of political representation, women's Islamic activism is clearly felt across the city. Paradoxically, women's marginalization offers them a degree of mobility and a space for activism—circumstances that make Egypt an excellent venue for this study.

Being an Egyptian national and a native speaker of Arabic facilitated my access to the field and to various Islamic organizations run by women. But my presence was complicated by issues of my own subjectivities and of power relations implicit in the ethnographic "ritual of confession." Chandra Mohanty (1988) pointed out that researchers with a Western education promulgate discourses that also normalize and reinstate relations of power. In turn, relations of power not only influence the researcher but also place the researched in the position of other. Foucault (1979) uses this dynamic in his notion of the confession as a ritual of discourse in which the speaker becomes a subject of the statement while the other, who requires the confession, listens and becomes their arbitrator. The balance of power thus favors the authority of the one who questions.

In my fieldwork, these roles have often been juxtaposed, as I was not always the one asking questions. This exchange of power roles continued throughout my relations with the women of al-Hilal, enriching my fieldwork in many ways by heightening my own awareness. It also created a reciprocity absent in the linear relationship between the interviewer and interviewee common in ethnographic accounts. Joseph (1996) described a similar nuanced reciprocity that occurs in ethnographic fieldwork in Middle Eastern cultures by offering a model of a culturally sensitive feminist reflexivity in which the ethnographic process is characterized by the connective relations and porous conceptions of the self. My fieldwork pursued this reciprocal sharing of and collaborating in the process of knowing.

Feminist research emphasizes the importance of self-reflexivity and stresses that we are what we study. The acknowledgment of one's own interests, objectives, and biases must be an essential ingredient of field research. The processes from which one draws and makes meaning and how these in turn are discursively produced and create one's desires and subjectivities accordingly must lie at the heart of methodology. Learning to represent oneself, one's own multiplicities as a subject, and the ways in which one is in constant flux and "in process" is part of these methodological approaches. Conversely, postcolonial analysis explains how colonialism has created fragmented cultural hybrids through intercultural battles and ideological discourse. This makes postcolonial places into sites of "cross-cultural refraction" (Coleman 1998), producing layers of complex distortions and new combinations and subjectivities. An awareness of the porous quality of the self with a primary focus on the discursive processes that keep us in constant flux is what Gilles Deleuze and Félix Guattari proposed when they wrote

Anti-Oedipus. "To reach, not only the point when one no longer says I, but the point where it is no longer of any importance to whether one says I. We are no longer ourselves. Each will know his own. We have been aided, inspired, multiplied" (1983, 514). When we gain the ability to consider new possibilities, we can break the surface of normative discourses.

While my national background may have enabled my research in some ways, it has complicated other aspects of my fieldwork. Being part of a social and cultural system assigns particular identities, roles, and expectations. An awareness of the privileges as well as the limitations of these positions was central to my presence in the field. Taking a reflexive approach to the experiences to which I was privy in my research was critical to my interpretation of the events. Gayatri Spivak stated that "to confront them (*vertreten*) is not to represent them but to learn to represent (*darstellen*) ourselves" (1988, 288–89).

As a middle-class Egyptian, I attended a British language school as a child. It was previously run by a British administration until the 1952 revolution when a new Egyptian headmistress was installed. The rest of the staff was British. But by the time I was in high school, many of these teachers had moved back to England. An incident in my junior year was a telling occasion when the intersection of the various social and political elements in my schooling came together. That day, a close friend of mine, Niveen, came to school "covered," or wearing what is now known as a *khimar,* a long garment that hid her long hair all the way to her waist, showing only her face and her hands from underneath its cover. Faced with the unprecedented event of a classmate's veiling, everyone was stunned into an uncomfortable silence. Back in the 1980s, very few people we knew were veiled; most women who did wear a veil were elderly women who merely tied a scarf around their head. But here was a girl, who was only sixteen, defying conformity by wearing a *khimar* and sitting calmly behind her desk in class as if it were the most natural thing in the world. After class, the teacher took Niveen aside and called her parents to come and pick her up because she was not wearing her uniform. Niveen never returned to school after that. We never saw her or heard from her. Her parents, who were very Westernized Egyptians, tried, but to no avail, to invite us over to their house to convince

Niveen to take off her veil, but we were too confused as teenagers to get involved in something we could not understand.

We later learned that Niveen joined a "fundamentalist"[19] Islamist group and married a young man she met there. We never knew why she decided to make that decision or why she chose to take this turn in her life. All I remember is that we were made to feel fearful of having the same thing happen to us.

In the 1980s in Cairo, our social world frowned on Islamism. Religiosity was strictly private, and my friends' parents and my own—most of whom were socialists—rarely discussed religion. A confirmed secularist, my father gave me only one piece of advice when I decided to do my research in Egypt: "Whatever you do, stay away from religion," he said. Being pious was a choice. You either pursued it or you did not.

To this day, my memory of Niveen and the way her life was transformed in a matter of months remain clear. Perhaps it was what eventually led me to work on women's Islamic activism as a way to understand the reasons behind her decision.

These memories lead me to ask today, What desires, yearnings, and longings compel a sixteen-year-old like Niveen to suddenly put on the *khimar* and devote her life to pursuing piety? And what desires instill fear in the rest of us, her friends and classmates, of such a choice? How do we simultaneously inculcate and cultivate these dichotomous desires? And more important, how do we sustain, fragment, and subsume these desires? I ask these questions because many years after the last time I saw Niveen, I stood in a small room in a suburb of Cairo with a group of Islamic activist women and shared with them the power of desiring. As a desiring subject myself, I continued to be keenly aware of my subject position as I came to know the women of al-Hilal and they came to know me. Throughout my fieldwork I was intrigued by the discursive distinctions of liberal modernity and Islamism that seemed to create a difference between me and them, but I marveled at the fluidity of our desires and how much we really shared with one another.

The organization of this book reflects my concern with the geographies of desire in Islamic movements. I use both a historical and a critical approach to presenting the ethnographic data because I also am concerned with why normative conceptual categories such as "religion" and "secularism" are diametrically opposed in analytical constructs, thereby obscuring processes of desire. In describing and analyzing women's Islamic movements in Cairo, I argue that desire cannot be understood outside the larger cultural and historical narratives, and I lay out these processes to situate the ethnographic data.

The next chapter, "Writing Religion: Islam and Subjectivity," critiques the implicit construct of "religious subjectivity" in the literature and its association with emotionality and irrationality in Western thought. Here I emphasize the development of scholarship that unproblematically links cultural assumptions to subject production. I explore how the nature of subjectivity develops as either "secular" or "religious" in Western scholarship by problematizing the binaries of Islam and secularity when viewed as separate and contradictory discourses. The aim of this chapter is to show that polemic categories of piety and secularism misrepresent women's desires in Islamic movements because such assumptions place them in a discursive space that they themselves may not claim.

Chapter 3, "Women's Islamic Movements in the Making," lays out the main themes in the historical processes contextualizing women's Islamic activism in Egypt. I examine modern state building processes, liberal reform, nationalism, and Egypt's open door policy up to the present. Chapter 3 provides the backdrop to the following chapters. Chapter 4, "An Islam of Her Own: Narratives of Activism," explores a variety of ethnographic examples and experiences from the al-Hilal's women's lives that reveal the inconsistencies, often disruptions, and ambiguities to provide a clearer, albeit complex, view of the multiplicities in women's subjectivities. My ethnographic analysis of Islamic activism exemplifies the goals and principles driving these women's movements. Chapter 5, "Desires for Ideal Womanhood," revolves around a number of case studies of women involved in Islamic activism at al-Hilal to drive at the ideals animating them at a deeper level. In these case studies, the combination of secularist and Islamic principles can be seen as part of women's ideals of Muslim womanhood. Chapter 6, "Development and Social Change: Mehmeit," recounts al-Hilal's development project in a village that I call Mehmeit. Women's experiences of activism are at the center of this chapter, which highlights their attempts at economically and socially developing a destitute rural community. Their development ideals mirror the principles of liberal secular modernity and offer a tangible example of the concomitance of these so-called binaries of religion and secularism. Chapter 7, "Reconsidering Women's Desires in Islamic Movements," concludes with a discussion of the significance of understanding subject production as processes embedded in specific historical and cultural contexts. This approach is paramount to explicating the ways by which "religious subjects" change, shift, and reveal inconsistencies.

As pious women in Cairo become involved in Islamic movements, they manifest complex and multifaceted desires mediated by Islamic religious and secular principles that shape their actions and construct their experiences. I interpret the actions of Islamic women by distinguishing their desires and analyzing the processes that produce and reproduce them. To misconstrue the desires and subjectivities of Islamic women by polarizing religion and the political project is to misread these women's activism and the nature of their movement. Understanding how desire and the production of subjectivity inform Islamic women's movements in the contemporary Middle East is of central importance in interpreting the modern configurations of power and social change of global dimensions in the world today. As the world grapples with issues of "religious fanaticism," "extremist politics," and "rampant violence" that seek justification in either "religious" or "secular" discourses, this book offers a vantage point that challenges these constructs and reveals the multiplicity in subjectivity and desire of the Islamic women activists who transcend the discursive boundaries of piety and politics each day. The implications of these research findings are significant in the current context of globalization and the contemporary modern era.

Writing Religion

Islam and Subjectivity

The Oriental is irrational, depraved (fallen), child-like, "different"; thus the European is rational, virtuous, mature, "normal." But the way of enlivening the relationship was everywhere to stress the fact that the Oriental lived in a different but thoroughly organized word of its own, a world with its own national, cultural and epistemological boundaries and principles of internal coherence.

—Edward Said, *Orientalism*

The central aim of this chapter is to challenge binary representations of subjectivities engaged in religious practice, as opposed to those who appear to engage with secular endeavors. This goal rests on the critique of assumptions that unquestioningly employ—as a marker of modernity—a universal distinction of religion as a separate category from other spheres of social life. Such sweeping generalities inform how foundational scholarship in the social sciences contends with issues of "religious subjectivity," representing the religious subject— a unit of analysis—as the antithesis of the modern subject, through which the principles of rationality, responsibility, and freedom are epitomized. My purpose is to trouble the most basic analytical constructs against which desires and subjectivities in Islamic movements are plotted.

Despite the critical impact of Said's *Orientalism* (1978) on scholarship dealing with Muslim and Middle Eastern cultures, deeply seated assumptions surrounding Islamic practices and Islamic actors persist.

Whereas Said urged scholars to think beyond cultures as "watertight compartments whose adherents were at bottom mainly interested in fending off all the others" (1978, 348), religious movements are decontextualized and uprooted from their historical logic. Most of these movements are framed as Said elides, as encapsulated, isolated, and preoccupied with staving off competing ideologies: "If it can be said that the modernist ideology of the post-Enlightenment West effectively separated religion from public life, then what has happened in recent years—since the watershed Islamic revolution in Iran in 1979—is religion's revenge" (Juergensmeyer 2001, 66). Conversely, an examination of the historicity of analytical categories of religion, politics, culture, science, and economics reveals that if there is indeed a "revenge" of any sort, it is the revenge of power structures that the Western modernist ideal of separating church and state has been unable to quell, indeed has rekindled in alternative forms.

The ethnographic data on women's Islamic activism in Egypt presented in this book demonstrate the inadequacy of prevalent conceptions that dichotomize liberal secular modernity and religion. These binary constructs persist today in views of "Islam" and Islamic intellectual traditions as being congruent with the medieval scholasticism beyond which the West has progressed, hence precluding any contextual analysis of religious participants. In this chapter, I consider the notion of "religious subjecthood" as fashioned by assumptions deeply embedded in Western traditions of modernity. I argue that these representations of "religious subjectivity" rest on liberal modernist principles of thought that normalize the strict separation of religion from the public stage of the political sphere. This approach, however, affords only a partial glimpse of the multifaceted desires and heterogeneous subjectivities of the actors who engage in Islamic movements today.

This chapter begins by tracing the general outlines of the history of religion as a separate category in social science scholarship about religion and religious practices that set the stage for the study of Islamic beliefs and societies. I explore how these trends inform and rationalize views of religion as the "other" of Western modernity. I also consider two case studies from France and China, which help describe an approach that overcomes the analytical limitations of liberal secular epistemologies. The latter assumes a bounded (having boundaries) nature of subjectivities that engage with religious practice and therefore limit our understanding of the heterogeneity of subjecthood. Constructing religion as a distinct category from history and place in the analysis of religious movements directly affects how subjecthood is conceptualized in them. I maintain that subjects are seamless and fluid and far more layered than some sources on religion make them out to be. Overlooking the interplay between normative conceptions of religion and other aspects of social life ignores the diverse ways in which desire and subjecthood are constituted and shaped, both historically and discursively.

Birthing Religions: An Exercise in Reproductivity

The concept of religion as it developed in Western thought is embedded in particular knowledge claims and power relations that must be unpacked in order to gain a closer understanding of the study of religions. The Western origin of the social sciences (such as anthropology) and their grounding in Western history, culture, and politics have led a number of anthropologists to move from studying "the other" to dissecting the Western project. Paul Rabinow calls this the process of "anthropologizing the West" (1986, 234).

I begin by analyzing the conceptual tools that created the hegemonic framework for thinking about subjects engaged in religious practice. In short, I anthropologize Western scholarship on religion, religious movements, and specifically those addressing Islamic cultures and societies. I begin with the individual who experiences, embodies, and actively participates in religious movements around the world and then turn to the socially productive: mothers, fathers, workers, citizens, intellectuals, poor, rich, and urban or rural.

"Religion" emerges as a central critical element in early Enlightenment thought. The confrontation between state-building projects and local elite powers in Europe justified their claims in religious terms. The rejection of religious paradigms of knowledge in favor of scientific observation and evidential inference marked the advent of not only the dominance of science but also the growing significance of the idea of secularism as the antithesis of religious authority. The Enlightenment period of the seventeenth and eighteenth centuries that developed through social, economic, and historical processes in Europe saw the crystallization of the modern concept of religion. The history of the English civil war (1642–1651) and the French Revolution (1789–1799) are two examples demonstrating the confrontation between religious ideological power and an emerging ruling class bent on new state-building plans. Consequently, an understanding of "religion" as a category that opposed and endangered the emerging European states remained tied to a notion of conflict and defeat in Western thought (Asad 1996).

Fear, incredulity, confusion, and superstition are identified by a number of thinkers and philosophers of modern religion as the point of departure for understanding the religiously faithful. David Hume (1711–1776), now considered one of the founders of the Enlightenment philosophy of religion, stated that "the first ideas of religion arose not from a contemplation of the works of nature, but from a concern with regard to the events of life, and from the incessant hopes and fears which actuate the human mind" (1757, 27, quoted in Morris 1998, 141). Hume is known to have emphasized the role of emotions in giving rise to religious belief. He argued that emotions like fear and the instinctive tendency of humans to "adulate," and not divine intervention or rational reason, were the compelling motivation behind popular religious belief. During the Enlightenment, religion began to take shape as an emotional, irrational, and antiscientific human condition that was seen to fill the void left empty by unexplained scientific knowledge. Ironically, despite their roots in social and cultural events pertinent to Western history alone, these descriptions persist in scholarship today.

Religion and the Religious Subject in Modern Social Science

Modern European thought that mirrored a concern with religion in these earlier views crystallized as a cornerstone of analysis of religious social phenomena. European philosophers described religion as "the opium of the people" (Marx, 1818–1883), "irrational" (Freud, 1856–1939), or "masochism" (Nietzsche, 1844–1900), thereby reinforcing the assumption that religion belonged to the realm of emotion and irrationality.[1] These views regarding the nature of religious experience can be described as almost a pathologization of religious feeling. At the same time, early anthropologists writing about religion—including Edward Tylor (1832–1917), who is recognized for emphasizing the intellectual aspects of religion—contributed to the understanding of religion as not only the contradiction of science but also the backward other of modernity and progress. Although he ascribed a rational mode of thinking to the people he studied, he nevertheless still viewed them in light of evolutionary frameworks, locating religious belief at the lower spectrum of human progress. "Yet while these principles prove to be essentially rational," they were employed by "savages" and those who were "in a mental condition of intense and inveterate ignorance" (1958, 23). Although nonliterate societies were often the object of similar claims, these views can still be found today in accounts of religious adherents of various faiths.

One work that has greatly influenced the understanding of the subjective experiences of individuals involved in religious practices to this day is *The Varieties of Religious Experience* (1902) by William James (1842–1910). His views of religion as subjective experience urges a consideration of the individualistic approach that takes account of each experience as unique to the person experiencing it. In choosing to follow a psychological approach, James defined religion as the "feelings, acts and experiences of individual men in their solitude, so far as they apprehend themselves to stand in relation to whatever they consider the divine"(1979, 50). Nonetheless, James is often criticized for limiting the scope of his studies to his own experiences and, in general, to Western societies, thus disabling a comparative consideration of religious practices in various cultures. The greatest limitation of his approach, however, is seeing religion as residing solely in the individual experience and overlooking wider social phenomena, therefore narrowing the range of religious expression at both the local and global levels of society.

By ignoring social and historical contexts and focusing on the individual, James's work influenced contemporary analysis focused on the interiority of a closed world of religious individuals and, consequently, is inadequate in examining the interrelated fragmented, multidimensional world where each individual simultaneously resides. More important, his work—although it devotes much attention to the personality and nature of the individual—lacks a grounding in historical analysis. An emphasis on the interiority of religious experience does not fully capture the dynamic character of the Islamic women that I describe in this book. Concentrating on the interior individual experience limits the analytical lens that studies use to look at similar subjects of study. Desire, I argue, is not confined to the interior deliberations of subjectivity. In fact, I contend that the interiority of subjects cannot be seen as separate from their exteriority. Instead, they are mutually productive and inform one another. Understanding the desire for religious piety, devotion, or activism as inhering in one's interior deliberations isolates these deliberations from the wider fluid geographies of cultural and historical forces that produce and shape desire. Moreover, understanding religion as a strictly individual experience is predominantly derived from the now universal assumption that religion exists in a bounded, private space that fails to take into account the porous nature of such secular notions of private and public and their contextual variations.

The grounding of the conceptual understanding of the religious in the interior world of individuals was all the more confounded by changes rooted in European history. These historical changes were to project a particular understanding of the "other;" the other non-European societies. The birth of anthropology thus came at a time when Enlightenment philosophy was also shaping ideas of Western intellectual and technological supremacy, a time when Europe was shifting its attention to what became its colonies in the East. A number of scholars have noted the relationship between anthropology and European imperialist agendas (Asad 1973; Mitchell 1988; Said 1978; Young 1995), showing how research agendas were fashioned through relations of power and colonialism, especially in anthropological studies of religion.

Anthropological studies from nineteenth-century European and American scholarship endorse the primacy of Western progress and modernity. Besides the technological advancement of Western societies that rationalized its implicit dominance, it was the assertion that non-European cultures were linked to superstition, magic, and religion and hence with tradition and backwardness. These societies were not to be studied in the context of their own histories but measured *against* those of Western cultures. The argument being made was to lay down the foundation of European colonization agendas and facilitate the construction of the backward "other" for centuries to come. The concept of religion born from specific European trajectories of history was the very carving tool that shaped the finite form of the "religious subject" in both Western and non-Western societies. The construction of binary oppositions between East and West, between the nonmodern and the modern, rationalized the discourse of the dispossessed ruled by their colonial masters (Said 1978). In anthropological studies of religion, scholars normalized these constructs of inequality in defining religion as a category of analysis that could be observed in nonliterate societies.

Confounding this situation was the fact that early anthropologists generally worked under the evolutionary premise that saw in primitive societies the origin of the present. Nonliterate societies were therefore used as a model of preliterate life to seek contemporary complex ideas in their simplicity. In keeping with the evolutionary paradigm and the emphasis on scientific rational thought valorized by Enlightenment thinkers, religious belief was understood to have developed from a so-called animistic faith to more rational belief systems. This explains the persistent division in the study of religions that Brian Morris (1998) describes as distinguishing between "folk" and "historical religion." Whereas a number of these early anthropological forays into the field of religion may have attributed to the "savage mind" an irrational and unscientific mode of thinking, this, according to Morris, did not extend to the same degree to the faithful of historical religions such as Christianity and Islam.

Despite these unquestioned assumptions, scholars nevertheless diligently pursued a working definition of religion. One influential work that contributed to these attempts was Émile Durkheim's *The Elementary Forms of Religious Life* (1912). Durkheim (1858–1917) defined religion as a separate category from everyday life, regarding it as "a unified set of beliefs and practices relative to sacred things, that is to say, things set apart and forbidden,—beliefs and practices which unite [into] one single moral community, all those who adhere to them" (1954, 37). His definition paved the way for anthropologists of religion like Clifford Geertz (1926–2006), whose work remains influential in studies of Islamic cultures and religion, to view religions as sets of symbols or structured systems. Durkheim's notion of religion lacked a more flexible understanding of society and its systems as complex, interrelated parts, but his emphasis on a unified body of a coherent and consistent structure can still be found in contemporary analyses of religious movements. Accordingly, individuals who participate in Islamic movements (such as the women of al-Hilal) are studied using an inflexible and anachronistic religious paradigm. Most of the literature analyzing these movements overlook the historical trajectories that shape the ways in which Islamic practices and secularization projects intersect and are simultaneously distinguished from one another. This absence of historical and contextual analysis tends to reify static notions of subjectivity that fail to account for the heterogeneous character of desire and the dynamics of the movements that shape them and, in turn, are shaped by them.

Unlike James, Durkheim was most concerned with the relationship between religion and society, so he moved beyond an individualistic depiction of religion. He located religious thought in the emotional state of the collective community and in its effort to come to terms with issues of uncertainty and disorder. Thus for Durkheim, the actor was almost always indistinguishable from the whole yet functioned in a stable and almost predictable manner. What appears as a parallel evident in Edward Tylor's and Émile Durkheim's analyses of religion is their assumption that "primitive man" was subsumed by the community. To them, action and intellectual activity were collective endeavors leaving little or no space for individuality, let alone the autonomous will so revered in Enlightenment rhetoric. To both scholars, primitive communities were synonymous with early human society. Viewed as communities ridden with fear and dislocation, they were represented as desperately clinging to the supernatural in the form of magic and ritual to make sense of their world. In this regard, James's and Durkheim's work reinforced the assumptions of their predecessors and continued to perpetuate an almost normative claim in the study of religion that "religious actors" were associated with emotional states, the supernatural as opposed to natural science, and that they were essentially part of a repressive community of collectively bounded believers.

It was left to Max Weber (1864–1920)—who declined to define the concept—to study religion as a system integrated in the spheres of society and economics. Weber wrote:

Religiously or magically motivated behavior is relatively rational behavior, especially in its earliest manifestations. It follows rules of experience, though it is not necessarily action in accordance with a means-end schema. Rubbing will elicit sparks . . . religious or magical behavior or thinking must not be set apart from the range of everyday purposive conduct, particularly since even the ends of religious and magical acts are predominantly economic. (1963, 1)

Here, Weber was attesting to the inseparability of animistic ideas from natural reasoning as "relatively rational." In that sense, he was referring to rational reasoning, not rational thinking. Therefore, although rubbing creates sparks, these early manifestations of human thinking in nonliterate societies did not include rational thought, owing to the nature of their beliefs. Weber assumed that rationality was linked to progress and, consequently, to the denial of magic and ritual in religion. To this end, he was unable to completely discard the normative belief that linked religion to irrationality, a fact that impeded a more nuanced understanding of the diversity of forms of rational thought among human societies and logical systems not contingent on merely the separation of religion from science and secularism.

Religious actors, however occupied a new space in Weber's work because he sought to understand the social function of religion not as Durkheim's moral glue of society or Marx's opium of the masses but as the comparative study of ideal types. Weber understood religious action from the *rational* subjective meaning of the actor. In that, he was influenced by Tylor. However, unlike scholars of religion before him, Weber maintained that the emotional factor in religion needed to be reconsidered:

At the present time, it is widely held that one should consider emotional content as primary, with thoughts being merely its secondary expression. Of course, this point of view is to a great extent justified. From such a standpoint one might be inclined to consider the primacy of "psychological" as over against "rational" connections as the only decisive causal nexus, hence to view these rational connections as mere interpretations of the psychological ones. This, however, would be going much too far, according to factual evidence. A whole series of purely historical motives have determined the development toward the supra-mundane or the immanent conception of God. (Weber 1958, 286)

Weber's integrational approach to the study of religion enabled him to consider rational reasoning as well as the emotional aspects of religious actors.

Subsequent investigations of the study of religion built on these trajectories, producing a richer debate in the field that based on the functionalist reasoning of Franz Boas (1858–1942) and Bronislaw Malinowski (1884–1942), A. A. Radcliffe Brown (1881–1955), as well the analysis of myth and the mythic structuralism of Claude Lévi-Strauss (1829–1902). The predominant goal of these studies remained tied to the pursuit of a definitive category that allowed an understanding of a cultural category of analysis labeled *religion* in accordance with the ethnographic method. That the category of what is known as religion appeared too diverse to be categorized or that the historical temporality of such understanding was too narrow did not figure significantly in any of these critiques.

Will the Religious Rational Individual Please Stand Up?

The question of rationality and religious belief was empirically examined by Malinowski, the founder of ethnographic investigation. Working from the idea that the ethnographer's role is "to grasp the native's point of view, his relation to life, to realize *his* vision of *his* world" (1922, 25, italics added), Malinowski studied the Trobriand islanders of the South Pacific, writing extensive treatises on the importance of viewing culture in context and not in the abstract. Despite his disavowal of the notion that culture must be compared with any future or past ideal in order to be interpreted, Malinowski's conceptual understanding of rationality nevertheless emerged from normative secular criteria. The limits of his ethnographic analysis in dealing with the variation in human subjectivity and the shifts between what was defined as public and private, rational and emotional, and political and religious may be attributed to the constructs of binary oppositions in its theoretical frame.

One of Malinowski's efforts was to dispel the assumptions regarding primitive humans' ability to reason. To disprove the theory of Lucien Lévy-Bruhl, which claimed that abstract thinking and systematic thought are not skills possessed by a "pre-logical mentality," Malinowski wrote, "We must surely pause before accepting primitive man's irrationality as a dogma" (1948, 9). Although he claimed that Tylor's ideas of animism attributed too much rationality to primitive man, Malinowski attested to the rational potential of the Trobriand islanders by demonstrating their ability to distinguish between what was mystical-magical from what was empirical-pragmatic, as he believed that the ability to be rational necessitates distinguishing between magic and science. Thus he assumed the separation of religion from science as a criterion for what constitutes rationality.

Malinowski cited ethnographic evidence that supported his thesis by recounting the Trobriand islanders' use of agricultural tools like axes and pointed sticks, their knowledge of the seasons and the soil, their rational treatment of death as a dispassionate ending of life, and so forth. He went on to argue that although magic was linked in some ways to their knowledge of gardening, its effects were not interchangeable with the effects of their labor; that is, the natives understood and knew that their crops were the result of their hard labor but that magic served to control the uncontrollable variables that might jeopardize their crops. Malinowski reasoned that in differentiating between the roles of the garden magician and the leader of the community, there was a clear separation between the rituals involving magic and secular leadership, yet these were, he admitted, occasionally carried out by the same person. Magic served to reinforce confidence in the face of adversity and was not conflated with logical outcomes. "It is most significant that in the lagoon fishing, where man can rely completely upon his knowledge and skill, magic does not exist, while in the open-sea fishing, full of danger and uncertainty, there is extensive magical ritual to secure safety and good results" (Malinowski 1948, 30–31).

Evident in the examples Malinowski cited to demonstrate the rationality of the native Trobriand islanders is his assumption that magic was separate from science. The distinction between what is religious and what is secular and scientific is where Malinowski looked for the decisive factor in determining rationality. Malinowski did not pursue the question of whether the Trobrianders had a word for religion, magic, or science as they are understood in the West. Malinowski's description of the rational actor was a product not of Trobriand beliefs and social ideals but of Enlightenment thought and liberal Western principles. Despite his intention to demonstrate the rationality of the native Trobriander, Malinowski succeeded only in reinstating the assumption of the binary construct of faith/reason and religion/secular. Consequently, Malinowski did not adequately challenge the notion of the traditional irrational individual often believed to belong to a nonliterate society. The reason is that he did not reject the assumption that *created* the irrational other as the religious backward actor, in comparison with the rational modern subject. An interesting idea that Malinowski did posit, however, is that ordinary people in both primitive and advanced cultures could entertain contradictory views at the same time. Malinowski questioned the extent of the subject's boundedness, irrational or otherwise. Although significant, his observation did not resonate with the anthropological interests of his time but picked up more momentum in later studies (Rapport and Overing 2000, 81).

When considering the activist women of al-Hilal, however, I had to begin with a clear awareness of the language they used to describe *din*, or religion, as opposed to Islam. To them, Islam and *din* were one and the same, and their difficulty in distinguishing between the two emerged from their practice of religion as a way of life. As they repeatedly told me, Islam permeated all aspects of their life. Thus, to separate *din* from their way of living, despite their normalization of Islam as an internal and private relationship with the divine, did not make sense to them. Their knowledge of Islamic teachings, which enabled them to experience religion as a lived tradition, still was inconsistent with modernization schemes enforcing a separation between religion and politics. But to them, the two were not contradictory.

In my conversations with Laila, who had been an activist at al-Hilal for the last five years, she made various references to religion as a "kind of science." In fact, on more than one occasion, she emphasized the meaning and order that Islam had brought to her life. Laila explained that like "science," Islam was a rationale that enabled one to understand one's self, limits, emotions, and desires. She emphasized that in the process of "becoming" a devout Muslim, which is always an incomplete and never-ending process, she had turned to religious teachings to "make sense of things."

> My duty is to always consult him [meaning God, or Allah] in all that I do. But this is not automatic. When you are angry or stressed, the blood vessels in your body contract, and the level of stress hormones rises in the blood; these are physical reactions to anger. You learn to accept them, and you also learn to overcome them. Islam helps me do this. It allows me to put things in perspective. To be calmer, at peace, when something bad happens, because you have belief in God. I am convinced that Islam is suitable for all time, that you can deal with it accordingly as a kind of science [in] that the more you discover in it, the more this science grows.

Although Laila never quite says it, she implies that as a rationale, Islam does not refute or challenge science. In fact, to her, *Islam is like a science.* What she specifically alludes to is that both are rational disciplines and both enable her existence, yet nowhere in her account does she perceive science and Islam as opposite or separate. What is more significant is the fact that they both merge in her words and neither is accorded a separate or reified logic. As religious actors, the activist women of al-Hilal engaged in debates drawing on complex ideologies and discourses that merged and intersected with their discussions of Islamic teaching. From the modernizing values instilled by nationalist states to scientific discussions of astronomy, some of whose roots are in Islamic civilization and sustainable development, these activists were able to master a heterogeneity of discursive traditions that informed how they understood their place in the world.

The data I collected from these conversations and observations of the al-Hilal activists pointed to the need for a theoretical lens that did not restrict my understanding of religious desire and subjectivity. I also could not push heterogeneous, complex, and varied desires that defy and challenge unitary interpretation into culturally and temporally specific analytical categories.

Geertz and Asad on Religion: Symbols and Power

Clifford Geertz's theory of religion as a symbolic system was an important trajectory in the study of religion in anthropology. Seeking to contextualize, interpret, and read symbols and meanings, Geertz (1926–2006) expanded on theoretical assumptions ingrained in Western thought, viewing societies as coherent universal symbolic systems, with religion clearly demarcated from other aspects of social life such as government, science, and common sense. His classic conceptualization of symbolic religious systems is "a system of symbols which acts to establish powerful, pervasive, and long-lasting moods and motivations in men by formulating conceptions of a general order of existence and clothing these conceptions with such an aura of factuality that the moods and motivations seem uniquely realistic" (Geertz 1975, 90).

Although Geertz regarded religious beliefs as both expressing a world order and shaping it, his treatment of religion as a hermeneutic tradition did not adequately explain the social forces behind the production of religious belief. Geertz unquestioningly accepted the discursive formations masking the actual power relations that created the category of religion. To show how Geertz's analysis was driven by Western categories of thought that distort his representations, Talal Asad (1993) related the genealogy of Geertz's interest in symbols and interpretation to the creation of secular discourse. Relying on Foucault's notion of confession, Asad showed that the development of this religious practice as a social norm disciplined society as a whole in medieval Europe. He argued that confession relied on a notion of truth that is linguistic and emerged from an exterior expression of interiority. It was from this interiority that religion came to be defined as belonging to the realm of inner meaning that explains Geertz's favoring of belief and symbolic meaning in cultural systems (Asad 1973). Asad then showed that the institutional dis-empowerment of Christianity by secularism and science motivated Geertz's analytical position, which takes for granted the separation of meaning from power.

Rather than pursue the forms by which modern institutions standardize knowledge, Geertz narrowed his focus to the symbols of religious systems. Because secularism defines itself in opposition to its own construction of religion, a consideration of symbolic systems alone does not explain the systems of representation taking part in their creation. That is, Asad's Foucauldian genealogical approach avoids sequential thinking, enabling an exploration of the complex and multi-layered shifts of history and power that demonstrate the inadequacy of the unilineal frameworks commonly applied in studies interpreting the religious movements of the Middle East and the Islamic social world.

In his analysis of the powers and ways of life that influence Western understandings of religion, Asad notes that critiquing the use of categories like "religion" and "secularism" as abstract, universal terms standing outside particular historical traditions is difficult. In fact, he insists that describing categories that exist beyond the normative boundaries of liberal language is limited by language and translation. Instead of viewing the secular "as the space in which real human life gradually emancipates itself from the controlling power of 'religion' and thus achieves the latter's relocation" (2003, 191), he demonstrates that the idea of the modern state itself produces the distinction between secularism and "religion," thereby justifying the state and occluding other forms of community. He then shows that the freedom of religious practice and belief is tempered by the condition that it does not impinge on the secular state's science, law, or politics. Arguing against such normalized categories in scholarship, he asks how, when, and by whom the categories of the religious and the secular are defined.

Reproducing an Idea of Islam

Any serious analysis of religious traditions needs to be sensitive to the processes of power, which makes some discourses possible and others obsolete. An approach that takes account of the historical complexity of discursive formations is helpful to understanding the underlying structures of power and their role in shaping the conceptual tools that scholars use to interpret religious practices and beliefs in the societies. I have selected two examples of scholarly treatments of "Islam" to illustrate that insufficient attention to issues of power can often turn religious traditions into ahistorical and isolated concepts and practices. My first example is John Esposito's work, because of its huge impact on the current literature dealing with Islamic studies. My second example comes from Mark Juergensmeyer's treatise on religious fundamentalism. His analysis of religious actors illustrates how notions of irrationality, violence, and intense levels of emotion are often normalized in the discussion. Labeling religion as a universal and anachronistic category is an exercise that subscribes to a particular cultural vision and whose futility is its unquestioning point of departure. It is not merely how we define religion, and consequently religious activism, but how we recognize religious activism when we see it. What epistemological processes inform the cognition of religious activism as separate from other forms of activism?

As I pointed out in the opening of this chapter, religious critics of state-centered liberal projects in Europe were identified as fanatical adherents of a superstitious creed who stood in the path of progress. In the late nineteenth century, with this discourse firmly rooted in their history and culture, colonialist European powers ventured into a predominantly Muslim world in the Middle East. Rationalizing their superiority as a modern force against an Islamic resistance, deemed intellectually unjustifiable because of its association with a religious ideal, the colonialist discourse readily constructed Islamic tradition as a "religion" that was (predictably) antimodern and irrational (Asad 2003). This transplanting of concepts, particularly that of religion, uprooted from their own histories and firmly lodged in the heart of an alien context, reformulates them into new discursive meanings. Local concepts are uprooted not only to erase any historical consideration of their development as part of logical matrixes of social life but also to strip them of credibility as viable discourses and to envelope them in a shroud of timelessness and "tradition." As concepts with no history and no context, they are transformed into ahistorical "symbols." Neat and compact, these symbols then act as vehicles of meaning that, on demand, conjure up the connotations they are intended to portray. According to this process of appropriation, concepts like "Islam" are born into a new world, divested of their historical meaning and cut down to size, to serve the purposes of hegemonic power structures in their new locale. Colonial discourse has been successful in doing this principally because these concepts are no longer made historically viable.

This is precisely why Asad (1996) calls for a consideration of Islamic tradition, not as a stage in social development measured against Western historical experiences, but on its own terms. This approach is not without its difficulties, however, because Western liberal modernity is presented as a neutral and universal ahistorical arbitrator. Western liberal modernity relies on an absolutist position whose bedrock is the inseparable treatment of ethics and rationality in its philosophy (MacIntyre 1988).

To varying degrees, these processes of decontextualization characterize how Islamic movements are theorized by social scientists today. One prolific writer on Islamist movements over the last two decades is John Esposito, whose work has influenced countless studies of the history and culture of the Muslim world. Esposito's work illustrates how current attempts at explaining Islam may nevertheless reify categories of thought that prevail unquestioned in the literature.

In his book *The Islamic Threat* (1992), Esposito attempts to dispel certain misconceptions of Islam. His analysis of how Islamic states responded to global politics relies on a series of typologies, which, although intended to demystify, it obscures as it organizes the data. To represent the range of diversity among Islamic states and debunk labels of fundamentalism and conservatism, Esposito further reinscribes and encapsulates Islamic states as types: "Saudi Arabia is a conservative monarchy, Libya a populist socialist state headed by a military dictator. . . . Pakistan under General Muhammad Zia ul-Haq embodied a conservative Islam, and Saudi Arabia still does; Islam in Libya is radical and revisionist; clerics dominate in Iran" (Esposito 1992, 28).

Although informative, Esposito's historical survey of Islamic thought applies a homogenizing lens on the various events that constitute this history from the eighteenth century to the present. His intent, which was to dispel misunderstandings of Islamic tradition, would have been better served by delineating its multilayered genealogy. Esposito's point of departure is based on his view that Islam runs counter to modernity and that Islamic movements in the Middle East emerged as a result of the failure of secular nationalist agendas. Despite challenging critics of Islam and Islamic cultures, his work belies a tendency to categorize religion as antimodern and opposed to progress.

Esposito's extensive scholarship alludes to the colonialist past only with regard to its cultural impact while glossing over the layers of ideological and discursive manipulations of a colonized Middle East. The scope of Esposito's contribution to the subject of Islamic movements and societies has had a long-term impact on how the subject is approached by various scholars. Despite making wide contributions to debunking myths about Islam and Islamic traditions, this body of literature continues to reflect a steady adherence to a fixed category of religion produced by a history of Western nation-building processes and colonial endeavors.

From a modernist perspective, Middle Eastern societies are viewed in their totality as "traditional" because religion still plays a role in the public sphere, which leads to the idea that these states are failed projects of modernity. However, the presence of religion in politics is growing in many countries around the world, where historical and political processes structure diverse conceptualizations of the public sphere.

In Egypt today, secularism and religion can be clearly seen as conflated and imbricated categories to which the sharp demarcations between secularism and religion in Western terms prove inaccurate. The permeability of the public and the private also challenges applications of analytical categories of "religion" as bounded and unchanging. On the one hand, Islamization is sweeping the public sphere; women's Islamic movements continue unperturbed; and political Islamic parties remain marginalized from parliament. On the other hand, the freedom of secular thinkers is tempered by religious power as well. The case of Nasr Hamid Abu Zeid, a secular scholar whose tenure was not renewed at Cairo University because of his secularist views, demonstrates that the sanctioned public role of Islam cannot be ignored. He is now in exile in the Netherlands after being legally sentenced to divorce his wife, since it is against Islamic law for Muslim women to marry nonbelievers. Although the state denies Islamic parties the right to represent themselves in parliament, owing to their religious nature, religious authority exercises a notable influence on the public sphere. That is, marginalization from the political process does not necessarily mean that religious power does not contribute to politics. Mutual interests traverse the seamless boundaries between the private and the public spheres and between the state and Islamic groups.

To interpret the global rise of conflict between religious movements and nation-states, a number of scholars have adopted analytical models that attempt to reconcile religious zeal with nationalism. The sociologist and political analyst Mark Juergensmeyer uses the term "religious nationalism" (2001) to describe what he understands to be a social phenomenon across the Muslim world. To Juergensmeyer, religious nationalism is an ideology that combines faith in a social order ordained by the divine with a modern vision of a nation-state government. According to his reasoning, some patterns in the wide range of religious movements around the world develop in distinct stages. They often begin with despair over a secular nationalism that clothes political aims in religious garb. Juergensmeyer calls this process "religionizing politics," and it is followed by identifying the enemy, a stage leading to religious zealots' pointing to secularism as a religious foe. Juergensmeyer cites Hamas and the Iranian revolution as examples of these groups "satanizing" the United States as the ultimate enemy of their cause. Finally, Juergensmeyer proceeds to stage 4, "the inevitable confrontation," which, he claims, is a natural outcome once the foe has been identified. After listing many such confrontations, Juergensmeyer tries to demonstrate that violent confrontations are inevitable because "there is a certain logic at work that makes this conjunction natural" (2001, 459). Violence, he explains, is religiously justified to adherents of these movements by means of images communicated through symbol and myth. The cross and the sword are examples he cites, because to him, they have associations with divine power and are almost always associated with violence. In an interesting interpretation of the symbols of violence that lie at the heart of religious traditions, he writes,

> These religious acts of pure violence, although terribly destructive, are sanitized by virtue of the fact that they are religiously symbolic. They are stripped of their horror by being invested with religious meaning. Those who commit such acts justify and therefore exonerate them because they are part of a religious template that is even larger than myth and history: they are elements of a ritual scenario that makes it possible for people involved in it to experience the drama of cosmic war. (2001, 459)

What I find most interesting in this quotation (and in the rest of his article) is Juergensmeyer's choice of words. The following terms intersperse his account describing both the state of mind and the political aims of these religious groups: "*against modernity*" (454), "why they *hate* secular governments with such a *virulent passion*, " (455), "they often *loathe* their own kind" (455), "For that reason they may *hate* not only the politicians in their own countries but also these leaders' political and economic allies in lands far beyond their own national boundaries" (455), and "the *anger* of the Serbs" (456). What is obvious from these accounts and the particular model that Juergensmeyer uses to interpret global religious violence is that he uses Western modern liberal rhetoric, which sees these movements as emotional, antimodern, antisecular, and, most important, irrational manifestations of religious zeal that just happen to erupt in these areas of the world owing to their local historical and traditional past. Absent is an analysis of the wider global contexts and historical background for each of the movements he names. Absent as well is any attempt to question how violence is defined by the state and how nation-states have indeed already perfected this "sanitization" of violent symbols in the military.

Moreover, Juergensmeyer's account reflects an unquestioned assumption that regards the nature of religious movements as the binary opposite of secular and modern nation-states, pitting each reified entity against the other. The terms "religious nationalism" or "religionizing politics" do little to resolve the issues, which are the separation of religion as a distinct category from politics and the liberal assumption that breaching this distinction causes violence, disruption, and war. The fact that the religious actors, the participants in these movements, are described in terms that hark back to the history of European religious wars in which the emerging state's religious opponents are constructed as backward fanatics is too obvious to ignore. In sum, Juergensmeyer's attempts to interpret religious movements are limited by his theoretical framework, which employs normative analytical categories. The subjectivities of individuals who participate in religious movements or practices, as in Juergensmeyer's account, inevitably assume irrational proportions and are constructed as the opposite of those associated with secular practices. This account is based on the strict binary categorization that views secularism and modernity as the antithesis of religion.

Next I turn to religious movements in China and France to illustrate how an approach not wedded to the normative demarcation between notions of religion and secularism can produce a more nuanced understanding. By problematizing these binaries and avoiding the normative tendency to classify ethnographic data, studies of religious movements can more adequately illustrate the contradictions and fragments that fall outside the analytical box.

Falun Gong in China and Religious Patchworks in France

Anthropologist Andrew Kipnis studied religious movements in post-Mao China (2001) showing how the state and religious activists negotiate different definitions of "religious activism" (in Western liberal terms). Religious movements and practices have recently proliferated in China, and Kipnis explains that what the state sanctions as religious is still limited to the main institutionalized religions: Christianity, Judaism, Buddhism, Islam, and Daoism. Furthermore, contemporary religious groups must define their movements as either Buddhist or Daoist or risk legal persecution if they are categorized as nonreligious superstitions. That is, these religious groups must obtain official permits from the state in order to "exist." The alternative is to be categorized as antiscientific and deemed irrational.

Falun Gong is a movement started by Li Hongzhi in 1992. But it is problematic for Kipnis, who explores where to place it as a category, since Li Hongzhi claimed that Falun Gong was not a religion but a form of spiritual cultivation. This claim has placed him and Falun Gong under pressure from the state and has attracted intense media attention. Labeled as a cult by Western media, Falun Gong continues to be difficult to categorize by all those involved. Kipnis concludes that since these religious movements do not contradict science or the state, they should be allowed to exist as "religions" as long as they proclaim a distance from politics and remain in a bounded space. Yet Kipnis does not explain why the activism of Falun Gong and the followers of Li Hongzhi should be placed in an analytic box. Although he attempts to escape the confines of Geertz's definition of religion, Kipnis somehow remains true to the normative secular-religious binary in his analysis.

The second case I present here demonstrates that an approach that problematizes the dichotomy between the religious world as confined to the private and the secular world as belonging to the public can be misleading. In France, religious activism has recently and increasingly attracted public attention. Although scholars have remarked on the growing numbers of the "unchurched" in Europe, particularly in France (Berger 2001; Dobbelaere 1981; Voyé 1999), Liliane Voyé (1999) observed that individuals now resort to what she calls a "religious patchwork." Religious patchworks use existing resources to construct religious experiences that best serve individual interests and needs. Voyé pointed out that the situation described more than two decades ago by Karel Dobbelaere, who maintained that secularism had not reached its zenith in Europe. Voyé states that the status quo cannot be described as being at the pinnacle of modernity. Arguing that even though institutional religion may not be able to dictate its views, she shows that the demonstrated ability of religion to act as a solution for contemporary problems has gained wider public credibility. Voyé noted that because the state not only tolerates this new role of religion but also sometimes seeks it, the role of the church has intensified in secular state administrations. This all is taking place in the context of what Voyé describes as "advanced modernity," in which science has come to have "perverse effects" that the state cannot control or regulate except with help from the church. For example, the Catholic church in France now acts resourcefully in situations from which it had once been marginalized.

Ethical issues, Voyé argues, once belonged to the domain of the religious actor. But because this changed with the advent of secularization, the individual is no longer able to define ethical parameters. Yet in today's France, issues of religious tolerance requiring ethical arbitration call once more on the Catholic church for advice. For instance, Voyé noted that Belgium, France and the Netherlands employ what is officially known as "ethical commissions" to deal with bioethical problems. Voyé thus sees the role of the church as changing. It has been "de-dogmatized" and "de-confessionalized" and, rather than speaking about the law of God, now focuses on human rights and human values. She cites Niklas Luhmann (1990), who uses the concept of "performance" to describe instances when religion plays a role outside its realm. This often occurs when religious authorities can offer help that the society or the state cannot provide. Voyé sees this as a significant change in modern thinking. Her observations of the shifts in French society and the newly mobile nature of the church, which permeates the private and the public spheres in the secular state, attest to the current seamless character of religion and secularism.

Although Voyé does a convincing job of showing that this case represents an important development in French society, it cannot simply be taken as the failure or success of modernity's ability to encapsulate and manipulate religion. The reason is that Voyé normalizes the separation of religion from politics as a requirement of modernity. This analytical limitation precludes the interpretation of the changing locus of religion and, consequently, potentially inciting more changes. According to Asad (2003), when the state sanctions the public presence of religion, it becomes a vehicle of modernity and not an attack on it. The changes in the role of the church and the private religious practices of individuals, however, produce subjects that may be acting as "free listeners" to religious activism in the public domain, meaning that religious rhetoric may become comprehensible to secular political audiences. Ultimately, this will have implications for the nature of the discourse taking place in public in France, as it will shift to accommodate and reflect these changes.

Scholars of religion often debate the extent to which hegemonic definitions of religion dictate interpretations of religious practices and beliefs (see Bowen 1998). Religion, which is often defined as a bounded social category, determines how studies shape and inform our knowledge of the "subject" involved in religious practices. Data collected from the field do not always adequately address the notion of "religious subjectivities," owing to the lack of a critical interrogation of normative conceptual binaries of secularism/religion, reason/faith, rational/irrational, and modern/traditional. Instead, the subject is viewed in terms that reflect an underlying opposition between a reified emotional religious subject and a scientific secular subject.

The themes discussed in the current literature on religion in this chapter show that universalistic analysis that fails to problematize the historical context of analytical terms eschews representations of desire and subjectivity in religious movements. Uncritically applying the normative construct of religion to these movements can obscure the historical and regional variation in Islamic practices. Normative claims regarding the irrationality and emotionality of subjecthood in religion are often distorted and inaccurate.

The ethnographic data on women's Islamic movements in Egypt presented in chapters 4, 5, and 6 of this book contradict the theoretical assumptions that gloss over the nuances in religious movements and activism. Although these normative beliefs guide some of the scholarly work on Islamic subjectivity, my findings show that the desires of women activists in Islamic movements in Egypt are shaped by various social, political, and economic processes that reflect concomitant principles of Islamism and secularization and a multiplicity of imbricated desires. Attempts at separating these strands embedded in Islamic women's desires results in reifying essences and leads to inaccuracy. Tracing how representations of "religious subjects" are discursively shaped by these normative concepts, I argued that power cannot be uncoupled from discursive representations of religious traditions. Early anthropological understanding of the subject involved in religious practice is derived from the concepts and assumptions that have historically defined religion and its place in Western societies.

The emphasis on separating secularism, science, and rationality from religion in Western history informs the binary opposition between religious and secular subjectivities assumed in the literature. As historical categories of thought, they are powerful tools for ordering the world and the people who populate it. The danger has been in the universalizing nature of these sweeping generalizations about religion and its followers. The implications of these assumptions for the analysis of subject production, in both Western and non-Western societies, are immense. The associations of religion with irrationality, emotion, and backwardness run through many early studies noted in this chapter: Tylor, Durkheim, Weber, and Malinowski set the stage for studies that often deal uncritically with religious activism and Islamic movements.

3

Women's Islamic
Movements in the Making

> We also have to start from a deep-rooted conviction that
> Islam calls for modernization, development, and keeping
> up with the spirit of the times. It is a religion that is built
> on tolerance, fraternity, compassion, and not causing
> harm to others except in the case of self-defense.
>
> —President Hosni Mubarak

Whether by acknowledging religion or denying it, various interlocutors author religious movements, drawing on historical and discursive processes that reinforce power structures in society. These processes of discursive production take place locally and globally, forming a discourse that is always in constant dialogue and is always responding to shifts in power relations. In the previous chapter, I traced a number of epistemological themes in the analysis of religion and the normative concept of religious subjectivity in order to highlight their limitations in studies of religion. I now turn to analyzing the relationship between the projects of secularization instituted by colonial and nationalist politics in Egypt and the production of secular liberal citizens of the state. Women are positioned at the intersection of these relationships. Simultaneously bearing the symbols of tradition and modernity, they continue to be the target of ideological projects that shape Egyptian social values.[1] Islamic women's activism embodies these trajectories, yet it also reconstitutes them in ways that reflect the inconsistencies, temporalities, and discontinuities in the mutual embeddedness of religion and secularism. An understanding of Egypt's particular historicity will shed some light on the processes shaping the desires of the women who engage in Islamic movements.

Islamic Movements in Egypt

The rise of Islamic movements as part of the religious resurgence around the world has sparked intense controversy and interest, particularly in Western discourse, in which Islamic revival is often represented as a monolith acquiring the proportions of a global tidal wave threatening to engulf the tenants of liberal democratic life, indeed of modernity itself.[2] Although the complexity of Islamic revival means that it cannot be described as a monolith, interpretations of Islam, Islamic movements, and resurgence have led to views that essentialize the multiethnic, politically diverse, and historically, culturally, and socially heterogeneous Muslim world. Dubbed by the media as the world's fastest-growing religion, Islam's 1.4 billion followers come from such geographically diverse areas as Saudi Arabia, Indonesia, Macedonia, and the United States. Muslim cities such as Cairo, Tehran, and Jakarta team with diverse, contradictory, and ubiquitous discourses, all of which proclaim to be Islamic. But it is often one "Islam" that persists in the Western imagination today, one linked to the underpinnings of stagnation, tradition, and even terrorism.

Seen as a global discursive shift after the collapse of the Soviet regime, "Islam" is posited in these views as the paramount opposing force to the current neoliberal global capital. Egypt's shift toward the Islamization of public life in the twenty-first century is clearly visible.

Often shunned and repressed by the government, the Muslim Brotherhood is Egypt's most popular Islamic group. Although its members generally uphold a philosophy of nonviolence and focus on social services to the poor, the Brotherhood has occasionally engaged in exchanges with the state that have often turned violent.[3] In Egypt's 2005 elections, the Brotherhood formed a political alliance with the secular left-wing party al-Tagamou'. Both groups rallied for the liberation of Palestine and called for common goals for the Arab region. In an unprecedented success, the Brotherhood, with its long history of providing social services for the masses, secured 20 percent of the seats in parliament.

These successes for Islamist groups have forced subtle shifts in the Egyptian government, which has remained a persistently secularizing state in character, if not in practice. Indeed, the Egyptian state regards

Islamization as a threat to national security and often propagates the idea that it is protecting the public space from incursions of blind faith and the "backward" "irrational" tradition of Islamist fundamentalism. This fact should not be taken at face value, however, as the Egyptian state continues to demonstrate an inordinate ability to negotiate and manipulate issues related to Islamist groups that has allowed the ruling regime to retain power. But the state has consistently conceded to the demands of Islamic groups in issues relating to women or the private domain of the family, according to Mervat Hatem (1986), in exchange for the Islamists' endorsement of the state.[4]

Although staunchly secular in principle, state discourse often reveals a subtle ambiguity vis-à-vis Islamism and avoids ideological confrontations with religious leaders whenever possible, preferring to issue public apologies rather than engage in direct dialogue. The resulting public discourse in Egypt is negotiated between the secular hegemony of the state and the growing popularity of religious groups like the Muslim Brotherhood, which, although ostracized from the political process, are confident in their ability to Islamize the Egyptian street and to win its support (Hatem 1986). Commenting on the marginalization of the Muslim Brotherhood from the recent invitation for a *hiwar*, or discussion, between opposition parties and the dominant National Party, Saad al-Hosinee, an engineer and member of the Muslim Brotherhood, commented, "This invitation does not cause any worry for the Brothers because they draw their strength and credibility from the Egyptian street first, which in turn appreciates the role of the Brotherhood because of what the group offers them and [the group's] noble message" (Adeeb and Ebeed 2009). This vexed relationship between the state and its only significant rival, the Muslim Brotherhood (although there are about twenty-four political parties in Egypt today, few if any are truly representational or have a significant following), constructs a seemingly binary public discourse. In fact, the give-and-take negotiations, some coercive and others diplomatic, attest to the mutual production of the country's sociopolitical environment. Numerous examples demonstrate this ambiguity in Egypt's public discourse.

In 2006 Farouk Hosni, the former minister of culture in Hosni Mubarak's government, was forced to issue a public apology as a result of comments he made opposing women wearing the veil in Egypt. He also had to agree to coauthor a book on the veil with Egypt's Islamic university, Al-Azhar, because he was said to have questioned the tradition of veiling off-camera in a television interview. Conversely, in October 2009, Sheikh Tantawi, the dean of Al-Azhar University who previously held the important position of Egypt's grand mufti, created a public uproar when he ordered a young female student at a Cairo school to remove her face veil, calling it "unIslamic."[5] It is interesting to explore these positions on veiling and to note the similarities in attitudes toward women's Islamic dress (Hosni was referring to the veil covering the hair, and Tantawi was pointing to the face veil). What is even more interesting is that religious figures like Tantawi often toe a middle line between what the ruling regime finds acceptable as religious markers and the limits of tolerance that the religious Muslim community will accept. Hosni, however, does not enjoy such liberties. As a secular and public figure who had only recently been the minister of culture, he cannot make such comments, not only because he is not a religious specialist, but also because he does not identify with the "religious street" in Egypt. Most notable about these exchanges is the absence of the voices of the women whose garments are being debated in the political forum.

Notable among other markers of Islamization is the widespread popularity of veiling among women in urban centers such as Cairo and Alexandria. The *hijab*[6] has become a highly coveted commodity in fashion centers in the city where veiled women shop for trendy Islamic dress. Fashionably veiled women are shown in newly established magazines such as *Jumanah* and *Al-Hijab Fashion*. *Al-durus al-diniyah* (religious lessons) are now widely attended by young and old, rich and poor. They are held in mosques and Islamic centers and are so popular that one of the *du'ah* (preachers), Amr Khaled, caused traffic to stop outside the mosque where he was giving lessons because of the huge number of people attending. Khaled later left Egypt after being allegedly harassed by the state. Religious lessons have also spread to sports clubs and private religious gatherings in homes and even to funerals.

An independent Islamic theater opened in Egypt in 1992 that calls itself Al-masrah al-Islami (Islamic Theater). According to its main producer and writer, Ahmed Abu Heiba, "The vision presented by our theater is the way art should be, congruent with religion and the traditions of society" (al-Bardini and Dabsh 2009, 1). The company is made up entirely of male performers because it does not approve of women acting on stage. Music and dance are not part of this "alternative theater," as some critics call it. Islamic theater performances address current issues of corruption and political concerns. Critics' reviews have been quite positive, with many predicting that it has great promise as an alternative to the deteriorating, state-sponsored, and privately funded theater (al-Bardini and Dabsh 2009).

Other popular performing arts include the *nashid*, a religious chant now quite popular at events like wedding celebrations, which extols the virtues of the Prophet and the greatness of the divine. Once reserved for Islamic gatherings and specifically to incite Islamic fervor, the *nashid* has now developed into a commercial art form sought out by newlyweds and the general public. Many *nashid* tapes are widely available even on supermarket shelves.

A number of scholars link these manifestations of religiosity to a superficial consumerist culture. Patrick Haenni and Husam Tammam (2003) labeled them "air-conditioned Islam." Although they are inaccurately generalizing a wide array of Islamism in the country as air-conditioned—meaning that it is an inauthentically acclimatized Islam—Haenni and Tammam do identify a new brand of Islamism. Comparing it with the "Western New Age religiosity" (a syncretic, decentered, and membership-free spirituality), they claim that this new phenomenon is driven by syncretic adoptions from other spiritual traditions. "Air-conditioned Islam" offers new healing and spiritual approaches and even uses yoga and reflexology and encourages the consumption of macrobiotic food. Haenni and Tammam link these practices to a new market economy that thrives on Islamic consumerism and is favored by a disenchanted middle class. Others (e.g., Starrett 1998) observed earlier that this trend was connected less to economic processes than to modern education and the state's ideological control over the schools' religious curricula. In his ethnography conducted in Egypt, Gregory Starrett explains that the literate population's ability to read Islamic scripture has allowed the public to counter the state's hegemonic control over the official Islam. "Putting Islam to work" to challenge and disrupt existing discourses thus has shifted the public's support from a state-sponsored Islam to a more individualized approach to religious practice. More than eight years after Starrett's study, the public's access to religious teachings through school curricula produced by a modernizing state has allowed thousands—men as well as women—to pursue what Starrett named an "enlightened" Islam. This "enlightened" Islam directs its adherents' social existence and shapes their experiences of selfhood to intersect with postcolonialist educational values largely unchanged since the British administration of Egyptian politics.

In line with this reasoning but taking the argument to the earlier years of British colonialism, Timothy Mitchell (1988) contended that colonialist administrations inculcated ideals of European liberalism to discipline the Egyptian mind and body by means of a civilizing project that worked through state institutions and apparatuses such as the school and legal systems. These modern liberal values are exemplified in the regimentation of schedules, personal hygiene, tidiness, punctuality, obedience, and discipline. Institutions of social control such as the military, schools, and hospitals introduced European ideals of bodily discipline that defined processes of subject production through the census, registration, health, hygiene, and law.

Despite political independence from Western colonialism, developing nations rarely change their educational systems substantially (Ashcroft, Griffiths, and Tiffin 2003). Even after independence from the British, modern liberal forms of social control and especially educational institutions continued to propagate the values of liberal modernity through a national identity that framed these ideals in local discourse. In contemporary Egypt, Islamic movements are complicated by these interwoven principles as the individuals who participate in these movements are honed by disciplinary processes. The kind of Islamism that has emerged in the Egyptian public sphere today, though as varied as it is complex, reflects this mutual embeddedness of discourses and practices.

After almost a century of British colonial rule, which started in the nineteenth century, Egyptian society has been restructured through the reordering of law and ethics to regulate the Egyptian population. Although the postcolonialist nation-state has adopted liberal modern principles as the impetus for these reforms, these ideals are imbricated with forms of religiosity not isolated from the secular public debate.

The historical record demonstrates these tensions and imbrications that have merged in Egypt's modernization saga.

The state's modernizing schemes could not have been possible, however, Talal Asad argues (2003), without the secularization of the *sharia*. The privatization of religion was one of the first steps toward creating the modern subject. Just as "religion" is trimmed to fit this new space, modern governments define its limits as well as the extent to which it can manipulate people's lives. Relegated to the private sphere and ideologically separated from the political sphere, the private spaces of schools and homes structure the religious experience and simultaneously produce subjectivities that internalize a limited public role for religion. Secularization projects in Egypt shaped its discursive history of Islamic practice. Yet these projects' inconsistent character, as Mitchell pointed out (1991), simultaneously provide space for Islamic movements to creatively maneuver the state's hegemony over public discourse. Accordingly, we cannot speak of subjectivities apart from the processes of secularization and Islamic discourse. Our understanding of secular and religious actors cannot be through a binary lens that perceives strict essentialist boundaries between opposites. Consequently, women's religious participation, the subject positioning they assume, the discourses they enable, and those they reject cannot be adequately understood apart from the processes of secularization and religiosity that shape them and their desires.

Women's Islamic movements in Egypt are among the notable contemporary social phenomena that negotiate these public discourses. Aside from nationalist activism against the British, there is not a single cause in Egyptian history around which women have rallied with such fervor. The rich history of the women's movement in Egypt has not paralleled, however, the vast appeal of Islamic activism that cuts across socioeconomic, educational, and age boundaries. Political analysts in Egypt have remarked on the similar success of the Muslim Brotherhood group in the last decade, attributed to the absence of a democratic political system in the country. As a result, marginalized Islamic groups such as the Brotherhood have become the uncontested voice of the dispossessed in Egypt (Nafaa 2006).[7] Analysts maintain that by secretly recruiting and raising funds, the Muslim Brotherhood has exploited the state's increasing hegemony over the public sphere, the absence of credibility of state agendas, and the state's elimination of political competition to gain popular support in Egyptian society.

Some writers in Egypt today argue that women's Islamic movements are merely part of the Muslim Brotherhood's well-established tradition of social reform, and that once more women are exploited as tools for political gain. Accordingly, they describe Islamic resurgence as a detriment to women's progress in the Muslim world and often name the resurgence as the main stumbling block between Muslim women and their liberation. In light of these generalizations, women's engagement in Islamic movements is perceived as the product of nonliberal religious practices and beliefs and therefore further contributes to the detriment of women in the Islamic world.

The agenda of the women I came to know in my own research in Cairo was independent of that of the Brotherhood. Although the thousands of women who join Islamic activist groups to promote Islamic social welfare may have mobilized because of the absence of other civil activist groups in the country, this does not explain the appeal of Islamic activism to Egypt's diverse population of women. Whereas their agendas pay special attention to women's role in society and in the family, the Brotherhood often claims that a Muslim woman's foremost role is in the family. But most of the Islamic women activists I have known maintain that this is not so and that the woman's role varies depending on each family's priorities.[8]

The ways people negotiate and rationalize their public experiences and actions as they engage in Islamic movements need to be reexamined. Although the feminist literature that represents women in the Muslim world as private actors has been widely critiqued, the fact that Islamic women activists act publicly, using what is often perceived as a "private" paradigm, compels us to reevaluate normative understandings that associate them with a specific rhetoric and fail to represent them as actors moving seamlessly through public and private spheres. The attempts to confine the role of religion by secularizing regimes in Egypt and limiting *shari'a* law to personal status laws has not succeeded in keeping religion out of the public domain. In Egypt, the role of the family is central to the organization of social life, and as the "entrusted keepers" of the family, women often act as the mediator between the secularizing and modernizing projects of the state and the family.

The most powerful force in Islamizing the Egyptian family today is women's Islamic activism, a fact that has intensified the Islamization of the Egyptian public. Yet social change whose organizing principle is the Islamic faith is the product of inseparable values of modern liberal projects that have historically shaped and, in turn have been shaped by, Islamic discourse and activism and desire.

With their two centuries of activist work, Egyptian women remain devoted to improving their status and roles in society. They work to develop Egyptian society itself, seldom pursuing their rights apart from an imagined ideal of Egypt and its future. Like religiously affiliated groups that, because of their associations with a "private sphere phenomenon," are marginalized from the political arena, women have had to work hard in Egypt and the rest of the Arab world to counter these normative demarcations of special politics. Consequently, Islamic activist women may be viewed as being caught in a double bind, first because of their Islamic agenda and second because of their gender.

The "world" of al-Hilal's Islamic activist women is embedded in the history and politics of Egypt through an array of complex, disjointed, and multilayered intersections. To understand these women's desires is to understand the historical and cultural transformations that motivate them and also to account for multiplicities in individual agencies as they negotiate, confront, and avoid hegemonic power. An important factor in disciplining the bodies of the Egyptian public is modernizations' particular emphasis on girls' education. My assumption here is not that these historical processes inculcated uniform, continuous, and consistent projects of desire in women's subjectivity but that these shifting layers of postcolonial modernities created geographies of desire that cannot be captured as a single or unitary subject position.

To capture these processes, I follow a number of themes in this history: modern state building, 1800s–1922; nationalism, reform, and Egyptian liberalism, 1923–1952; and independence and nation building, 1952–1970s.[9] The period from the 1970s to the present is marked by "an open door," or *infitah*,[10] resurgence of Islamism and the solidification of state control and civil unrest. A more detailed analysis of the mutual embeddedness of secularism and religion in Egypt warrants a separate study; I offer only an outline of this relationship.

Modern State Building, 1800s–1922

The arrival of Muhammad Ali (1769–1849) on Egyptian soil marked the beginning of an era of modernization and state-building projects that continued for almost a century of Turkish dynastic rule. Ali's reforms included the restructuring of Egypt's economy and army as well as its social, religious, and educational institutions, with the aim of sustaining political power.

According to Timothy Mitchell, these reforms were intended to "infiltrate, re-order, and colonize" (1991, 35). He argues that as the country was thrust into a new modern order, the government began its centralization, secularization, and bureaucratization. In the nineteenth century, Egypt sought to regulate social behavior and labor production by instilling in the population a fixed sense of time and space, order and obedience. The establishment of a comprehensive educational system encompassing both primary and secondary schooling and the European training of Egyptians was intended to produce the new, individual citizens of the state, disciplined and productive subjects. Placing the religious 'ulama[11] on the government payroll extended the government's control to religious schooling, which enabled its secularization. The educational system adopted the "model school"[12] as an ideal, and Europeans oversaw "modern" schools in the cities. Although religious education in the form of kuttab[13] was denigrated, it continued in rural parts of the country.

The state's modernization schemes, often aimed at limiting religious authority, gradually constructed a discursive binary between the progressive nature of state reforms and the "backward," "traditional" practices of the religious establishment. The 'ulama, whose authority was limited by these claims, regarded modernization as a form of Western imperialism and, not surprisingly, as a loss of Islamic culture. Several Islamic leaders—especially the proponents of Salafi Islam,[14] Jamal al-Din al-Afghani (1838–1897) and Rashid Reda (1865–1935)—actively pursued a return to a pure form of Islam unadulterated by Westernization. Anti-imperialist in its inception, the movement's most influential leader, al-Afghani, traveled to Egypt where his call for a return to Islam fired up many of the dispossessed *'ulama*. At that time, Islamic reform and activism were shaped primarily by the modernization schemes that sought to limit and defame religious authority.

On the economic front, changes early in the Ottoman period in Egypt signaled a shift to private ownership instead of state ownership, giving rise to a class of wealthy elites in the country. This burgeoning class of capitalist landowners, mostly of Turkish descent, continued their practice of maintaining harems, and their elite women were often kept behind its walls and wore face-covering veils when they went out in public. This had a wide effect on Egyptian society, as women's segregation became one of the markers of upper-class membership. Women from Egypt's lower classes, whose livelihood depended on farming and small businesses, suffered an even bigger loss as they, too, were effectively confined to the household, thus ending their access to markets (Cole 1981).

It was at this point, according to Leila Ahmed (1992), that the state decided to draw up plans for women's education. As a result, a school for training women doctors opened in 1832, and secondary education for girls began in the 1870s. Education was thus linked to social mobility for young women, as wealthy elite families began teaching their daughters European subjects, following the practice of Muhammad 'Ali himself, who had tutors teaching both Arabic and European subjects to his daughters and other young women in his court. 'Aisha Taymour (1840–1902), a famous poet and accomplished writer, was herself educated in this way. She was highly proficient in classical subjects, as well as the Arabic, Persian, and Turkish languages, and wrote poetry in all three. Her views on women and religion were radical for her time, as she argued that wives should disobey their husbands (and even leave home) if their husbands failed to carry out their obligations to them as listed in the Qur'an (el-Sadda 1999).

Whereas Egyptian women lived segregated under Ottoman harem life, they did not fare better under the British occupation (1882–1936), despite the latter's assertion of their support of women's freedom. Besides the traditional patriarchal system that continued to wield power over women, the British government assumed control over the male head of the extended family, which also influenced the treatment of women. The significance of the family unit in extending British control and its modernist ideals to Egyptian society cannot be overemphasized. Foremost among the processes structuring the family's experience of modernization and secularization was education.

Boys' schooling remained important to the modernization of Egypt, and girls' school education also received a rather significant measure of attention from the British authorities.[15] The reason was, as Mitchell (1988) shows, that girls were the gateway to the Egyptian family. The disciplinary values of bourgeois individualism important to the creation of modern subjects were inculcated in girls, who would later become mothers and maintain exclusive access to their children. As vehicles of modernity, these girls-soon-to-be mothers would raise offspring who were disciplined and industrious subjects of the state. Census taking, the introduction of health and hygiene in schools (Mitchell 1988), and child-rearing practices that foregrounded the superiority of scientific European pedagogy (Shakry 1998), as well as school curricula—all were means to that end. It was not that these practices were entirely new, "but their language and method aimed to eliminate an entire way of understanding personal vulnerability among ordinary Egyptians, particularly in the village, and to replace it with a nineteenth-century notion of the body."[16]

These reforms, however, were not without problems, nor were they intended for all social classes. Juan Cole (1981) pointed out that toward the turn of the century, as Western norms began to gain more ground among the upper classes, women in the lower petite bourgeoisie (*'ulama*, bazaar keepers, and artisans) continued to be segregated as a reaction to the growing European influence in the country, which was enforced by those resistant to Westernization. Cole reasoned that for the lower petite bourgeoisie, Westernization did not offer the same opportunity for economic gain as it did for the upper classes. Hence, the majority of Egyptians who did not benefit from these changes adhered to a course of authenticity and Islamism, drawing on practices of the earlier Ottoman upper class in maintaining harems.

According to Cole, toward the end of the nineteenth century, the impact of modernization schemes on women seemed to have created an ideological divide. In his analysis, whereas modern liberal emancipation was offered to upper-class women, an Islamically informed male discourse was bent on rejecting it for lower-class women. These perceived binaries were based on the colonialist discourses that made the local populations into an "other" and denigrated local culture and particularly Islam, which was constructed as the opposite of modern progress and a detriment to women (Said 1978). In this way, discourses of power facilitated the justification of the disciplinary processes implicit in the British colonialists' modernization and secularization projects and discredited the local populations' efforts to deal with these huge shifts in their lives.

Against such divisive rhetoric, several intellectual figures emerged in the mid-nineteenth century who dedicated their work to bridging such divides. The life work of the Islamic scholar Muhammad Abduh (1849–1905) focused on articulating Islamic thought that was compatible with modernity. He was influenced by al-Afghani, with whom he created the journal *Al-Urwah al-wuthqa* (*The Unbreakable Bond*), which was aimed at modernizing Islam and safeguarding it against European distortions. The British, who were aware of this anti-imperialist endeavor, plotted the organization's downfall and shut down the minaret that disseminated their views.

Abduh relied on *ijtihad*[17] to expand the reinterpretation of the Qur'an as a response to contemporary issues. He called for women's education and the end of polygamy—aims that influenced the work of both his friend Qasim Amin (1863–1908) and his student Ali Abd al-Raziq (1888–1966). Abd al-Raziq was an Azhar scholar who argued that Islam needed to be understood as a religion and not a state. The controversial message of his book *Al-Islam wa usul al-hukm* (*Islam and the Foundations of Governance*), which was published in 1925, led to his expulsion from Al-Azhar University. Among other things, he argued that Muslim communities should elect the type of government that served their immediate interests and their society, whether the ruling regime was either secular or religious. This assertion marked the point when the debate between Islam and secularism, or *al-'almaniyya*,[18] turned to authenticity versus Westernization.

Amin is known as one of the founders of the women's movement in Egypt, and his work on reform continues to stir up controversies to this day. *The Liberation of Women* and *The New Woman*, written in

1899 and 1900, respectively, maintain that Egypt's progress was contingent on women's emancipation. Amin used a modern liberal discourse of capitalism combined with references to Islam in his work. Although he called for reforms for women such as access to education and employment and the need to protect the family from the occasional practice of divorce, his views were limited in their scope for a real place for women in Egyptian society. Instead, he was more concerned with women's role as the mothers of future modern generations—a vision that served the purposes of the British occupiers. Amin was not interested in women's political rights, nor did he seek an emancipation for them that would reform patriarchal practices. He was more concerned with superficial changes that, following the European model, would transform Egyptian women from a general state of backwardness to a new condition of civilization. For example, despite severe criticism by the public, he demanded that women remove their veils.

Leila Ahmed concluded that although Amin sought to improve Egyptian society, he did so at the behest of women. Indeed, his upper-class bias drove him to seek reforms that served the needs of his own class (Ahmed 1992, 155–65). Moreover, Amin's otherwise celebrated work further alienated the growing Islamized petite bourgeoisie, who opposed his views. Likewise, the 'ulama rejected his vision of reform, which they deemed un-Islamic and called for the protection of women from the indignities to which Amin was subjecting them.

According to Lila Abu-Lughod's (1998) analyses, Amin's goals for women were unattainable, and they undermined rather than improved women's status in the country. The reason was that in imposing Western criteria on women's emancipation, Amin directed Egyptian feminist women to look beyond their borders for models of emancipation.

Despite these limitations, Amin's contribution to women's issues in Egypt had far-reaching effects in both Egypt and the Arab world. Egyptian feminists rallied around his ideas and soon took more public positions in calling for their rights in education and the right to worship as men do, in mosques. Malak Hefni Nasif (1886–1918) and Nabawiyya Musa (1890–1951) led the women's movement and during the 1919 revolution pushed for a new era for Egyptian women when they joined the nationalist party of the Wafd to bring an end to the British occupation.

Nationalism, Reform, and Egyptian Liberalism, 1923–1952

Even after two decades of hard work, Egyptian women were far from reaching their goals of holding office in the government or seats in parliament or even for suffrage. As women used their energy for writing and publishing, they succeeded in forming a tenable relationship to the public, which later created vehicles for their activism. By the end of the century, however, feminist resistance had, to a large extent, become nationalistic as women became concerned mainly about independence and emancipation from the British.

Several scholars of the Egyptian women's movements point to the twofold nature of its beginnings during these years. Leila Ahmed (1992, 169–88), for example, maintains that Egypt's feminists were either Westernized activists, like Hoda Sha'rawi, or were authentically Egyptian activists, like Malak Hifni Nasif. Fadwa el-Guindi noted about Hoda Sha'rawi that "despite her prominence as a feminist leader, she was distanced from her native language and therefore not a complete insider in her own culture" (1999b, 60). El-Guindi reasons that at the turn of the twentieth century, various factors such as pressures from colonialist powers, the spread of missionary education in Egypt, changes in consumptive patterns, and the secularization of Egyptian society led to the dismantling of these traditional forms of education that prevailed in the nineteenth century.

This linking of colonialism with Westernization and secularization is a familiar trend in various accounts describing Egyptian history as a deviation from the path of nationalism and authenticity into an embrace of the West and Western trends. An underlying assumption in the historical accounts of Egyptian women's feminist activism is that women's movements in Egypt fall into one of two categories, one that is Western and inauthentic and the other that is Islamic and hence "authentic," without problematizing the notions of authenticity, Islam, or secular Western relationships to Egyptian history and culture. As el-Guindi stated about Nasif and Sha'rawi:

> The two leading women espoused two feminist views: one more authentically Egyptian, the other Western-influenced. . . . The Arabic language and Islamic knowledge mattered to Malak Hifni Nasif,

but were not included in the official feminist agenda as it developed under the leadership of Hoda Sha'rawi, which stressed women's suffrage, education reform, health services, and employment opportunities. Nasif, in contrast with Hoda Sha'rawi, was highly proficient in the Arabic language. She gave lectures in fluent Arabic and was a prolific Arabic writer. She was comfortable with her roots and well grounded in her native [Arabic] language and Arab culture. (El-Guindi 1999b, 65)

Although el-Guindi concedes that the agendas of these two women had obvious similarities, she maintains that

clearly, whereas Sha'rawi was socialized into a world that attached high value to French culture above local tradition, Nasif was firmly rooted in Arab-Islamic culture. But one cannot easily characterize Nasif as a traditionalist. In their ultimate goal of advancing women's rights, Nasif and Sha'rawi did not differ. Had Nasif lived longer, however, it is very likely that two parallel-organized feminisms would have developed—one grounded in Arab-Islamic culture, the other in European culture and feminism. (1999b, 67)

What we can conclude, however, is that being Islamic is the antithesis of Westernization, as El-Guindi normalizes these binary constructs and assumes strict demarcations between Islamic, European, and feminist.

Labiba Ahmad was a contemporary of Sha'rawi and Nasif who, according to Beth Baron, took an alternative path to the secularism of the Wafd, which was favored by women activists, and instead espoused the "Islamic bent of the Watani Party" (2005, 189). Like the other proponents of women's rights, Ahmad included Egyptian nationalism in the struggle. Faced with a restricted place for women in the public domain, like others before her, Ahmad turned to publishing and social welfare schemes. Building on Islamic tradition, Ahmad's agenda adopted what often became a conservative stance on women's issues. Baron describes various instances when Ahmad criticized what was, to her, inappropriate public behavior, such as mixed bathing, sports for girls, and foreign schooling. Baron is careful to show that although she followed a clearly

Islamic path, Ahmad nonetheless adhered to modern ideals and principles of social reform. "That the domestic roles laid out for women in Labiba's Islamic ideology upheld the ideals of a modern bourgeois family rather than some 'traditional' or 'authentic' Islamic ideal is further proof of the modernity of her message" (Baron 2005, 202). In sum, although Ahmad is portrayed as opposing secular women's activism, Baron describes her as an Islamic nationalist. Because Ahmad's activism is observably modern and has nationalist leanings, it is therefore not "traditional" or "authentic" Islam. If not, what is Ahmad's position? Baron does not explain further. Such awkward positions—the binaries of Islam/authentic versus modernity/Western—in which analysts of women's activism find themselves are not restricted to Baron or to el-Guindi but are a troubling recurrence in the literature on women in the Islamic world. In fact, the entire body of literature on the phenomenon of "Islamic feminism" has yet to reach consensus on whether or not Islamic women qualify as "feminists."[19]

At this juncture in activist history, a new group of political players entered the scene. In 1928, the Muslim Brotherhood was established by Hassan al-Banna, who was very popular with the masses. Because he called for an Islamic state and rejected capitalist reforms and social manifestations of Westernization, his message resonated with the lower socioeconomic classes, which had been left out of the reforms of the last century. These people saw in al-Banna a leader they could follow, whose message they could understand. Most important, the Brotherhood's social activism had already left a favorable impact on the rural communities, which rarely saw a helping hand from the state. In contrast to the perceived corruption and "Westernization" of the upper class, al-Banna stressed morality and Islamist values and "authenticity."[20] But despite the Brotherhood's conservative views on gender segregation, male authority over women, and a tendency to keep women in their roles as mothers and wives, an important female member, who was to have a visible impact on Islamic activism, rose from its ranks.

Often labeled as an Islamic feminist, middle-class Zeinab al-Ghazali (1917–2005) founded the Muslim Women's Association when she was eighteen years old. Al-Ghazali is often cited as exemplifying women's Islamic activism because as an Islamist, she was deeply involved with the Islamic Brotherhood at a critical time in Egyptian history. Al-Ghazali was attending religious lessons at Al-Azhar in 1936 when she decided to start an organization of her own. She maintained her ties with the EFU (Egyptian Feminist Union), however, and later joined forces with them to promote nationalist activism. With the reputation as a "soldier of God" among Islamist women and men, al-Ghazali had a tremendous following. She established the framework for the Islamist movement in Egypt and is said to have regrouped the Brotherhood after many of them had been imprisoned. Indeed, her ties to the Muslim Brotherhood put her own safety in jeopardy. Despite having been courted by Gamal Abdel Nasser's new nationalist government before it assumed power, the Brotherhood was now being persecuted. In 1966, al-Ghazali was sentenced to jail, a subject of some controversy, since she claimed that she was tortured there.

When she was released by President Anwar Sadat a few years later, al-Ghazali's reputation assumed larger-than life proportions, and she remained popular until her death in 2005, at the age of eighty-eight. Her life's work was to spread the *da'wa*,[21] which she regarded as central to her Islamic duty.

Al-Ghazali maintained that Islam has no women's issues; rather, Islam views women and men in a unified sense with clearly defined roles for each. Al-Ghazali's views were based on gender differentiation, in which both men and women are equally deserving of divine blessing but the leadership roles should be reserved for men. Women instead are the nurturers, a role that she saw as central to society's overall health.

Her discussions of gender roles in the Muslim world are unfortunately often framed as a critique of Western societies, where such distinctions between women's and men's roles are not clear. To al-Ghazali, this practice is extremely harmful, first to women and second to society. But even al-Ghazali's views changed over time. Azza Karam (1998) noted that al-Ghazali's views shifted in the latter part of her life to accommodate a more agentive role for women. But al-Ghazali's life itself does not mirror these views, as Karam pointed out, since she was a well-known activist and worked without stigma with her male colleagues from the Muslim Brotherhood. Moreover, when her marriage impeded her activism, she was able to divorce her husband, since she had stipulated in her marriage contract that she had the legal right to do so.

One of al-Ghazali's compatriots was the feminist Doria Shafik, whose life took an important if difficult trajectory. Born into a middle-class family, Shafik received her doctorate in France. But on her return, she was soon disappointed by the EFU (Nelson 1986). In fact, Shafik's views were sometimes too radical for her time, and she lost the support of her compatriots. Although she dedicated herself to women's issues for the rest of her life, she was unable to accomplish all that she had set out to do. She staged hunger strikes, demonstrations, and sit-ins to call for women's right to run for parliament. But Shafik was not a skillful politician, and her alienation was costly.

Independence and Nation Building, 1952–1970s

The period after *al-thawra* (revolution) was an awakening of Egyptians and Egyptian hopes for the future of the newly independent state, Arab nationalism, and the crystallization of Egyptian national identity and pride. Under Gamal Abdel Nasser (1918–1970), the country made a visible shift toward nationalism. The government's political aims were now directed at a mainstream, both nationalist and socialist, discourse that excluded all others. Although women were not singled out for specific reforms, they also enjoyed the state's newly established rights and services. The government focused on public services as well as the basic needs of a population that was emerging from "backwardness" into the modern world. Education, health care, and social welfare were available to all. Despite the gains that women were now enjoying, the gender ideology that marginalized women from economics and politics remained unchanged. What was worse, the Islamic personal status laws still controlled domestic matters and were not changed by the new ruling regime. Despite attempts to establish a new kind of feminism, called "state feminism," which was intended to mobilize women, women's political roles remained largely unchanged (Hatem 1992).

The wave of nationalism and modernization came to a halt after Egypt's defeat in the 1967 war with Israel. This was an important milestone in Egypt's history, for several reasons. Most important for this book is that it provided the turning point for Islamic groups to emerge as a social and political source of comfort to the millions of people who lost not only loved ones but also their national pride and hopes for a better future. Even though the Islamists were persecuted during Nasser's administration and many fled the country or sought invisibility, they nevertheless mobilized in prison and in the diaspora. Their alleged plot to assassinate Nasser had cost them dearly, but they were able to revive their movement after the defeat. This time, however, rather than resort to violent tactics that they could no longer sustain, they changed their priorities to produce an intellectual and social legacy that would rival the state's and win the hearts and minds of the people.

Among the Islamist women who emerged at that time was Safinaz Qazim, who no longer has a following and is not involved in women's Islamic movements in Egypt. Few of the women of al-Hilal had ever heard of her. Even so, she represents a strand of Islamic activism that appealed to intellectual Islamist women, whose knowledge and opinions seldom find their way to the public forum. The fact that Qasim writes a weekly column, has access to the media, and is concerned with art and music is an indication of the kinds of Islamic expression that are afforded a place in the public and those that are not.

In the 1990s, women's Islamic activism grew exponentially. Much of the activism of women's Islamic organizations builds on the old tradition of social welfare services and activities like health care, literacy classes, arts and crafts, and vocational studies that people like Hoda Sha'rawi and Labiba Ahmad set in motion in the late nineteenth and early twentieth century.

From the 1970s to the Present

Immediately after he became president, Anwar Sadat (1918–1981) began implementing an agenda of his own. He released many of the Islamists imprisoned by Nasser and pursued a strategy of keeping his friends close and his enemies even closer. To do this, he continued to negotiate with Islamist groups, for whom his complacency with issues of women and the family guaranteed appeasement (Hatem 1986). Moreover, encouraging Islamist trends was Sadat's trump card against Egypt's secular left. During Sadat's presidency, he turned the economy from Nasser's socialist course to an open door policy that welcomed international corporations and foreign investment. A new capitalist orientation replaced the old, economically frugal agenda, and once again the Egyptian lower classes were left to cope with the new change. Because large numbers of laborers found themselves on a downward spiral of poverty, they sought work in the then oil-rich Gulf states, leaving behind families headed by women. New attitudes toward religion, emphasis on piety, and Islamic dress subsequently found their way into daily Egyptian routines, and as women learned to take care of their families on their own while their men labored abroad, gender roles shifted as well (Abdel Kader 1987). In addition, new attitudes toward the consumption of material goods mingled with imported traditions from the Arabian peninsula, as well as Western-ization trends imported by international franchise, swept across Egypt, as social attitudes toward nationalism, Arab unity, and independence gradually disappeared.

The final departure from the nationalist period and its take-no-prisoners attitude toward Israeli occupation came when Sadat signed a peace agreement with Israel, negotiated by President Jimmy Carter. This leap was a shock to millions of Egyptians as well as even more millions in the Arab world. Some commentators claim this was the last nail in Sadat's coffin as far as the militant Islamist groups were concerned. Others blame a picture of Sadat's wife Jihan waltzing with Carter in the White House. Whichever it was that signaled Sadat's end, the response was swift and very violent. On October 6, 1981, while watching a victory parade in Nasr City, Sadat was gunned down by army officers of a militant Islamic group known as al-Gama'a al-Islamiyya. Nemat Guenena (1986) described the trials of the assassins, which revealed the group's socioeconomic similarities: most were middle-class high achievers of rural background and specifically from Upper Egypt.

The assassination of several dignitaries seen on television appalled Egyptian viewers to varying degrees. Many who had noted the surge in extremist Islamist groups began seeing anything to do with Islamism as a threat. Both militant and nonmilitant Islamists, such as members of the Brotherhood, were hunted down and imprisoned. This dramatic turn of events and the historical trauma it caused Egyptian society turned many away from any sort of Islamic gathering or organization, regarding them with suspicion or even fear.

Not for almost a decade after these events did women's Islamic activism in Egypt begin to gain momentum. In the late 1980s, a woman from Syria arrived in Cairo with her businessman husband. This woman, whom I will call Warda, was to create the biggest network of women's Islamic activism in Egypt's history.

Little is known about Hagga Warda, a small woman in her fifties around whom hundreds of women rally. Very unassuming, she commands the awe and respect of the women who see in her an inspiration for their activism. The literal meaning of *hagga* is a woman who has completed the pilgrimage to Mecca, one of the five pillars of Islam. It is not a hierarchal term but a common respectful way of addressing Muslim women over fifty. Most of the women activists I have met talk about Hagga Warda as the founder of their type of activism. Rather than a leader, she is considered more as a symbolic figure who has a certain historical importance. Several branches of the organization that Hagga Warda developed in Heliopolis opened in other suburbs of Cairo: Helwan, Mohandisseen, Maadi, and Haram, all strategic locations across the capital. There are no branches in the administrative districts of Cairo, or the center of the town, *wist al-balad*. Instead, Islamic women activists chose residential areas for their organizations because they wanted them close to their homes and neighborhoods. Out of the main organizations located in the suburbs emerged *gam'iyat* al-Hilal.

The rapid increase in these organizations is often regarded as indicating the lack of state support for the growing masses who are increasingly more dependent on these organizations in meeting the climbing costs of living and the decreasing value of their wages. In 1992, Egypt had 3,554 religious organizations, or 31.4 percent of all civil organizations were religious in nature. By 2002, this number had grown to 34 percent (Kandil and Nafiss 1992).

Hosni Mubarak began his presidency almost three decades ago, and Islamism continues to spread, even faster. Mubarak's regime has stabilized some aspects of Egyptian life, including the economy. However, as years turned to decades, Egyptians are having more and more difficulty with the day-to-day logistics of maneuvering through traffic to get to work on time, paying bills in government offices, and even shopping for food. As state services decline and prices rise, with little or no change in the overall status quo, public demonstrations sporadically erupt. Factory workers, students, day laborers, and occupants of shanty towns continue to demonstrate against conditions that grow dire with each passing day. Corruption and increasing wealth among the elite have made matters worse. As the decrease in jobs in Arab countries has led to a rise in unemployment, younger generations have begun publicly expressing dissatisfaction with the government and the lack of opportunities for living a better life, getting married, and buying an apartment.

Rural workers looking for jobs flock to major cities in search for a source of income to support themselves and their families. Overpopulation (Egypt's population has jumped to 80 million) is directly undermining the infrastructure, which in many parts of Cairo was always inadequate. Twenty-two percent of Egypt's households are headed by women, with rates of illiteracy remaining especially high among females, who suffer from a lack of vocational training or opportunities for employment. The percentage of people living below the poverty line in Egypt increased from 17.1 in 1981/1982, to 24.2 in 1990/1991, falling to 22.9 in 1995/1996 and 16.7 in 1999/2000. Despite this, 10.7 million Egyptians are short of food and necessities, compared with 7.3 million in 1981/1982, which is an annual increase of 2.15 percent (World Bank 2002).

Egypt today is painted in Islamic colors. The streets of Cairo are decked with Islamic symbols and paraphernalia. Islamic dress, *al-zy al-Islamy*, and the veil are the most obvious indicators of the Islamization of Cairo's streets. Although these markers do not necessarily denote an increased religiosity among the Egyptian population, they do point to a public presence that cannot be ignored.

Many of the women who participate in Islamic movements find their calling in an Islamic ideology that offers them a feeling of participation in addressing some of their country's needs as well as fulfilling their religious inclinations. To these women, activism is not merely social welfare work or the extent to which they can change Egyptian society for the better. It also entails how they can put themselves at the center of these reforms. As Islamic subjects who desire divine approval, they pursue social and personal change in accordance with the Islamic tradition.

Social Change and Women's Islamic Activism

Representing women's Islamic activism as a religious sort of activism, philanthropy, or religious nationalism assumes a separation of Islam from politics and the history of secularization in Egypt. Hence, it is inaccurate to see these movements as either religious and pious and relegated to the mosque, or as social movements of no other particular character other than that they are Islamic.

The general task of anthropologists is to describe the ways of life, social practices, beliefs, and traditions of peoples and cultures. It is not groundbreaking to claim today that concepts central to the intellectual matrix through which social beings view and interpret their world, such as religion, should be explored in their wider sociocultural histories. Approaches that separate religion from other forms of social life do not take account of the complex ways in which Islamic activism permeates social spheres, regardless of how these spheres are defined in Western tradition. Moreover, in thinking about women's Islamic activism, we are faced with yet another challenge. This is the tendency to associate women with the domestic sphere and to separate them from the public political domain of Middle Eastern societies.[22] Conversely, modernization schemes in Egyptian history have consistently focused on religion and women.

One of the ways secularism thrives is through discourse that provides the language for secular activists to participate politically. But since religion is relegated to confinement, religious activists cannot participate in the public sphere equally, since they do not possess the "language" of secularism, and if they do speak for their rights to participate, they will not be understood. Both democracy and human rights use a secularist discourse that facilitates an engagement with secular subjects and marginalizes religious actors. In the Middle East today, the public realm marginalizes the political representations of religious groups in the electoral process and regulates their social participation. Islamic movements that are seen to be too political are often persecuted. But because of the permeability of the public and the private spheres and the importance of the family and its historical relation to Islam through the personal status laws, Islamic activism participates through and beyond these spheres.

Although deeply committed to raising awareness of the plight of oppressed women in the Middle East and elsewhere, feminist literature still fails to articulate their condition in ways other than the obvious dichotomy of state versus Islam or modernity versus tradition. I believe that the mutual embeddedness of Islamism and secularism enriches the exploration of the complex and multilayered process of women's subjectivities in Islamic movements.

4

An Islam of Her Own

Narratives of Activism

If I picked up a small pebble and threw it in a pond, it would create a small ripple that breaks the surface and then disappears in the larger body of water. But if you, I, and others picked up more and more pebbles, we would make waves that would change the boundaries of the pond. That is how I see what I do as being significant. It is not only that I try to be a better Muslim woman or raise my children well and do my job better, it is that I provide the force for part of this wave.

—Amira, an Islamic activist at al-Hilal

Women's experiences with Islamic activism in Cairo are at the center of my ethnographic account in this chapter. Through these women's accounts and my observations of activism at *gam'iyat* al-Hilal, I explore the desires and subjectivities of the activist women who work to Islamically reform Egyptian society. These findings reveal that the multiple variations in subject positionings cannot be attributed solely to a fixed and stable conception of religious disciplinary practices, namely, Islamic practices. Although the women themselves present their subjectivities as a consistent and homogenous unified whole, their accounts do in fact reflect inconsistencies, disruptions, and ambiguities that are linked to modernizing projects, in which the concomitant processes of secularism and Islamization shape and inform their desires.

Desire reflecting the mutual imbrication of secular and Islamic principles can be discerned as subtle, fragmented themes interwoven in the activities, discourses, and behaviors of the women who participate in the Islamic movement in Egypt. These fragmentary themes are difficult to discern, not only because they are subtle, but also because Islamic women activists are engaged in projects of Islamic self-formation that they define as distinct from secular and liberal personhood. Consequently, they narrate their life histories and experiences by intentionally distinguishing themselves from the trajectories of liberal secularism.

The slippages and ambiguities that I identify are those that the women normalize, which in turn enables a more accurate understanding of the rhizomatic desires that pursue no particular pattern or cohesion. One of these themes centers on the ways that Islamic activist women consistently define religion as a private category, reflecting the secularist principle that separates religion from public life. Their normalization of religion as a private phenomenon contradicts Egypt's prevalent position regarding Islamist groups, which openly desires political control and calls for the application of *shari'a* and an Islamic state, as well as the principles of women's own activism. Nonetheless, according to these women, they are not contradictory.

A second theme emerging from the data is that the activists' understanding of Muslim womanhood reflects the mutual embeddedness of secular agendas and Islamic ideals. Again, to the women themselves, this understanding is not contradictory or identified as such. Modern secular values emphasizing individualism, autonomy, freedom, and self-expression have merged with Islamic ethics of Muslim communitarian sentiments, selflessness, love for God, divine sovereignty, and submission to divine will. The third theme is the perceived divide between private and public, which is a secularist construct that the activists themselves have naturalized and applied to their understanding of religion and their activism. The fourth theme is the principles driving al-Hilal women's activism, which mirror various aspects of modern secularization projects and Islamic ideals.

These themes can be found throughout the following three chapters, but not in an organized fashion, thereby reflecting the inconsistency and variation in the discourses on subject production. My objective is to demonstrate that women's Islamic activism in Egypt today drives and is shaped by the participants' projects of self-formation, which intersect, interact, and fuse with the processes of modernization and secularization of colonialist and nationalist histories.

One of the challenges I face is that in order to clarify the mutual embeddedness of Islam and secularism in the activist women's desires, I risk reifying these discourses or presenting them as contradictory, even when the women of al-Hilal do not see them as such. I have argued that the dichotomization of religion and secularism is contingent on specific historical processes and is not an essential fact. Therefore, I avoid pointing out what seems to be Islamic or secular. Instead, in my analysis I refer to the historical processes traced in preceding chapters that enabled these concepts in desiring subjects. Moreover, I do not assume that a direct causative relationship exists between a historical event or series of events and a particular notion of womanhood, activism, or religion. Notions of womanhood, activism, and religion are discursively produced. Foucault would describe these processes as

> ways of constituting knowledge, together with the social practices, forms of subjectivity and power relations which inhere in such knowledges and relations between them. Discourses are more than ways of thinking and producing meaning. They constitute the "nature" of the body, unconscious and conscious mind and emotional life of the subjects they seek to govern. (Weedon 1987, 108)

These processes are therefore incomplete, partial, and discontinuous.

For the women who participate in Islamic movements in Egypt today, religion and secularism are linked to the processes of modernization aimed at transforming Muslim subjects into citizens of liberal democracies. As I pointed out earlier, when addressing Islamic movements today, key academic categories such as secularism and religion are limited as units of analysis, owing to the close ties between these concepts and particular Western historicities. A theoretical bias assuming an oppositional binary between religion and secularism is a powerful paradigm necessitating serious attention because it applies a fixed dichotomy between what has often been assumed to be "religious" and "secular" subjects that are normalized in the literature. I challenge this dualistic thinking by showing that Islamic women's desires reflect the inseparability of religion and the political project. I maintain that desire is highly contingent and fluid. It takes shape in the contexts of cultural hegemonies and national narratives of modernization as individuals negotiate and cultivate their own subjectivities and identities.

Al-Hilal, Organization, and Activism

The private voluntary organization of al-Hilal is housed in a large, nondescript, three-story building in one of Cairo's southern neighborhoods. Each floor in the building is equipped to offer a different service for low-income women—many of whom are single mothers or widows—and their families.[1] The ground floor is used as a day care center for children of poor working women, who pay only a modest monthly fee. A large space with shelves and long tables functions as a small library and provides a working space for children's art projects. A few rooms on this floor cater to children with special needs, training them in a range of activities to enable them to become self-reliant. On the second floor is a big, carpeted hall with large windows where prayers are held. Lessons in *fiqh* and *shari'a* take place there every Monday at 11 A.M.[2] Charity bazaars also are held in this hall, which provide funding for the *gam'iyah* and a venue for selling the articles produced in the vocational studies classes, such as frozen cooked meals, food products, baked goods, basketwork, beautiful handwoven oriental carpets, and handmade items, including towels and linens. Al-Hilal's wares are very popular with the neighborhood's shoppers because they are made from natural ingredients and, more important, those who purchase these products are fulfilling their religious duty of almsgiving. At least a few times a month, al-Hilal's held charity bazaars, and their products were consistently the first to be bought.

The third floor of al-Hilal's building contains classrooms, complete with blackboards and desks for the literacy classes held daily, the religious classes for schoolchildren on Saturdays, and their summer school classes. The hallways and doors are lined with bulletin boards that display students' work and are colorfully decorated with construction paper cutouts.

Gam'iyat al-Hilal was established in the 1990s with the help of donations collected from the community members. Al-Hilal is part of a network of Islamic women's PVOs run by women for women and with branches all over Cairo. Al-Hilal's annual revenue from donations is relatively substantial, usually 100,000 Egyptian pounds (roughly US$20,000). Al-Hilal is supported by a network of professionals, especially in medicine and pharmaceuticals, who offer their services to the center for free as a form of pious almsgiving. These services include health care, education, and government and administrative help in overcoming the hurdles of Egyptian bureaucratic red tape and facilitating many of al-Hilal's projects.

How al-Hilal began is part of the history of the *gam'iyah*. It is a story that I have heard on numerous occasions, in great detail, from many of the participants at the center. Hagga Afaf, one of the first women to work with al-Hilal's director, Doctora Zeinab, described it in this way:

> After spending ten years in Saudi Arabia because of my husband's work, we decided to come back to Cairo. Both of our kids were college age, and we wanted them to go to Cairo University. Soon I found myself at home in the suburbs and didn't know anyone. When I heard from some friends about Hagga Warda, who was giving classes in religion [*durus din*] in Masr al-Gadida [a suburb north of Cairo], I decided to go. I went and sat in on one of her classes. As time went by, I found myself getting more and more involved. It was the combination of learning about Islam and the social work that drew me to activism.
>
> I met Doctora Zeinab at Hagga Warda's in 1991. We decided to get together and invite other women to join us here in our own neighborhood. We knew we could do many things, and Hagga Warda encouraged us. We also learned a lot from her. In the beginning, Doctora Zeinab started giving lessons at the sports club, whereas I was more concerned with the administrative part. I organized the lessons and made sure everything ran according to schedule. We began giving the lessons with a group of close friends, and they brought more friends, and their friends brought their friends, and so on. It was the most wonderful time of our lives, as if we were tasting something sweet [*bindu' haga helwa*]. The taste of Islam [*ta'm al-Islam*].
>
> Doctora Zeinab found an empty building in this neglected part of the suburb. It was still unfinished. Even the walls were bare, and there were no floors and no windows. We started bit by bit; it was

just a huge job, but at the time that did not deter us. Soon, with the money coming in from people around this neighborhood, we got one floor ready. Five years later, we had finished another floor, and now look at us! We have this three-story building with hallways, classrooms, and prayer halls. We have a fully equipped kitchen to produce our food for catering, and we have arts and crafts facilities where women can come and learn how to be productive. I was there in the beginning with Doctora Zeinab. We built this together.

Hagga Afaf's use of the metaphor of sweetness illustrates the pleasurable sensation of pious devotion and Islamic activism. It is a poignant illustration of desire as a material sense. She also emphasized the women's collective achievement rather than her own personal achievement, a common thread that runs in many of the stories I heard. This not to say that individual achievement does not exist; Hagga Afaf obviously was proud in telling me this story, but her pride was not for herself alone. It was pride for Doctora Zeinab, who runs the center and is its spiritual leader whom she considers her teacher; and it was also pride for a love of Islam and how that love enabled them to create the *gam'iyah*.

The ethic of activism at al-Hilal has two objectives: the community and the love of Islam. The vision that inspires the activist women is the desire to become good Muslim women, both at home and in society at large. This vision is directly tied to feelings of religious devotion. It is a love that is produced in the women as they attend classes on Islamic teachings, acquire knowledge, and seek Islamic ways of understanding their link to the divine. It is reflected in their practices, in their relationships with one another, at home, and with those they help.

Most of the women who run al-Hilal are from the middle class described by Galal Amin (1997) as a socioeconomic level that has mushroomed since the 1952 socialist revolution. Educated and upwardly mobile, the Egyptian middle class supplies the professional labor for the private sector. A few of the al-Hilal women are from the upper-middle class, and the larger pool of volunteers come from various socioeconomic levels. But this does not mean that women's Islamic activism in Cairo is a middle-class movement or that being middle class is a requirement for leadership.

It is important to note, however, that the women leaders of PVOs like al-Hilal were the most educated or had work experience in a predominantly middle-class field.[3] Dina, a young activist specializing in the organization of and research for religious lessons at one of the satellite PVOs, explained how the leaders at the center were chosen:

> You have to earn your place in the center. Being reliable, punctual, and consistent in your attendance are the most important factors determining your value as a dependable volunteer. You also need to work hard at the religious lessons and do well on exams. It goes without saying that a good background in education will help you learn. *Fiqh* is sometimes very hard to understand. I have noticed that those who do well in discussions and on exams are those who are able to think critically. These people are university graduates like myself. Education determines how well you will perform in general because you can think logically.

The value placed on education at al-Hilal cannot be overemphasized. Education is a central value of liberal secular projects in Egypt, and it is also important to Islamic values and tradition. Although education is often cited as a means of "knowing" in itself, as a vehicle of religiosity, it also enables educated women to run a *gam'iyah* as big as al-Hilal efficiently. Education at al-Hilal is an organizational principle. The emphasis on critical thinking and logic is important to note, especially because Dina did not mention piety or religious devotion as a determining factor for leadership. Clearly, in al-Hilal's organization, a modern education is a requirement for assuming higher responsibility. Neither class nor socioeconomic level is as important to the organization. Although leadership requires a certain level of education, that is not the only criterion. Such liberal values of punctuality, achievement, excellence on exams, and the ability to think critically are desirable qualities as well in a leader at al-Hilal.

Many of the women I met at al-Hilal and other PVOs in Cairo were engaged in Islamic *da'wa*,[4] leading social development projects and attending religious lessons at al-Hilal. The more experienced of them were *da'iyat* who offered religious lessons to women and, like many other women preachers in Egypt, attracted much media attention, most of which was negative.[5] The Ministry of Religious Endowments (Wizarat al-Awqaf) certifies these female preachers, who draw thousands of city women to listen to their sermons. While not feminist in their orientation, many *da'iyat* do promote women's status in society as part of a larger project to educate the masses in the refined practices of Islam, which, in turn, is a means of changing society. Among the issues frequently discussed in these public lessons are *mo'amalat* (social behavior) and the ways these Islamic modes of behavior should be adjusted to perfect the self and draw closer to God. The general aim of these lessons is to encourage the women in the audience, who have varying socioeconomic, age, and educational backgrounds, to find in Islam a frame of reference and platform from which to confront the problems and concerns of an increasingly challenging, global world. The emphasis is not on a return to Islam, as the lessons I have attended by Doctora Zeinab and Shereen Fathi, a well-known *da'iyah*, show. Instead, their focus is on developing a contemporary dialogue with Islamic teachings, namely, a dialogue based on knowledge of Islam but going beyond traditional or rigid interpretations.

I went to hear a lecture given by Shereen Fathy, whose religious lessons are highly regarded by some of the activist women. She was to speak at a large mosque in Heliopolis, a neighborhood under construction and close to Cairo's international airport. It soon became apparent that the class would be huge, with about three hundred women attending. Everybody sat in rows on the carpeted floor as if ready to pray. In fact, some women were sitting on their prayer mats. No one stirred or talked. Cell phones were turned off. The women's attentiveness was impressive, unlike any I had seen in public gatherings in Egypt. Each woman had a notebook open on her lap, and some were taking notes. In addition, a small textbook was being distributed to each attendant by a volunteer at the door. That day, Shereen Fathy was explaining one of the Qur'an's verses. She sat on a raised platform, cross-legged and dressed in white as if going on a pilgrimage to Mecca. She exclaimed at the beginning of her lessons:

There is no *hayaa fil din* . . . !⁶

We cannot keep turning our backs on important issues that we face in our daily lives today. You all [pointing to the women assembled in the main hall of the mosque] must face the challenge of raising your children in the world of the Internet and cable television. The other day, a woman came to me with her teenage daughter. She was only sixteen. The mother was in tears. Her daughter had been deflowered [*faqadit 'uthryitha*]. She had committed *zina*.⁷ I took her in, embraced her. I listened to the girl, tried to understand her circumstances, and counseled her and her mother.

Then raising her voice as if to the heavens and all those would listen, "*Hal nuqim 'alayha al-hadd*?⁸ Of course not! This is not why we are here. We need to see these problems as part of the times we are living in and not be hasty in our judgments. Islam taught us to have mercy and to leave judgment to God alone."

Afterward, Shereen Fathi started the midday prayer by calling for the well-being of all Muslims and all humankind.

These were Fathi's words. I was stunned, as I am sure many others were. Here she was talking openly about *zina* in front of nearly three hundred women and basically taking quite a different tack from conservative male clergymen's view of the subject, many of whom would have answered yes to her question of applying Islamic *hadd*.

Like many other *da'iyat* in Cairo, Shereen Fathi comes from the middle class, the daughter of a military father whose family resides in Heliopolis, a suburb where President Hosni Mubarak also lives. Many military personnel who work in the nearby army headquarters live here as well. Fathi is in her late forties and graduated from Ein Shams University's medical school. After several years, she gave up her job as a doctor because she did not have time for both her family and her profession. Fathi maintains that she could not be "faithful" to two jobs at the same time and so chose the one she considered more important. The fact that Fathi defined her position as a mother and housewife as "a job" says much about her position on women's role in society. That is, she does not see the role of housewife as a natural duty but as a choice. Fathi speaks well. She explains her views clearly and knows when to pause for effect and when to raise her voice to make a point.

On another occasion when I went to hear her, she discussed women's duties and rights in Islam. Her religious talks always use familiar examples, anecdotes, and jokes to lighten up her lessons.

Doctora Zeinab, who runs al-Hilal, is similarly concerned with the problems facing contemporary Egyptian society, women's place in it, and their potential to effect change. On the several occasions that I have met with her or attended her religious lessons, she has emphasized her belief in the importance of women's productive role in society:

> I have always said that women can contribute to society . . . to improve the situation in Egypt. Women have the potential to be productive outside their homes. I am totally opposed to those who say women should remain at home. It is true that the family deserves most of our attention, especially now, but that does not mean that women should just spend all their time cleaning and cooking and helping their children with their homework. I tell you, get out. Get involved, even if for a few hours a week. Each woman can help others in whatever way she can. This is part of being a whole person.

> If women always stay at home, how would they be able to prepare their children to deal with modern-day problems like drugs? How could they have a good relationship with their husband if they spent their day only cooking and cleaning? No, I really see women as instrumental in dealing with today's problems of poverty and ignorance.

On another occasion, I heard Doctora Zeinab respond to a question about the struggling economy and lack of employment and whether the women entering the labor market would compete with men, who are expected to support their families. She replied: "Why can't both men and women work? There are so many different opportunities for women to be productive. Work is not just employment for a wage; it can also be volunteer and charity work" (Hafez 2003, 73).

Most women in the middle and lower-middle classes do not work outside the home, as they are neither driven by economic necessity nor belong to the upper elite class in which gender roles do not restrict women's desires. Instead, Doctora Zeinab was referring to ways for women to be productive rather than simply to enter the labor market.

Shereen Fathi and Doctora Zeinab epitomize the general attitude of other women I interviewed in regard to activism and women's role at home. That is, housework acquired a whole new different meaning when they became Islamically aware. It was not that they no longer valued their wifely and motherly duties or that they felt they needed to be involved in something bigger, but that their involvement in Islamic activism gave these actions a deeper meaning. Samya, who lives in a lower-class area of the suburb and whose husband works in a factory as a *mulahith* (supervisor), described her experience of housework as activism:

I used to be overwhelmed when I thought of all the chores I had to do each day. Waking up early with the children, getting break-fast ready, and seeing them off to school only to be faced with the housework, which I never seemed to be able to finish. I had no time for myself, no time to do anything. . . . But after I began working at the *gam'iyah*, everything I had to do before seemed easy, and I was finished with my housework in no time. By 10 A.M. I am done and ready to start my work at the *gam'iyah*, whereas before this the chil-dren would come home at 3 P.M. and I would still not be finished. It is incredible that when you have God in your heart, things just start to take on a different look.

I feel I am more organized now, whereas before I was merely going from one task to another. Raising my children is easier. Learn-ing how to listen to them and discussing matters with them [are eas-ier]. I learned all this here. Knowledge also is important; knowing is what matters. I learned *fiqh*; I learned about the women in Islam who came before me. I have a good grasp of all this because of the *gam'iyah*. Doctora Zeinab encourages me. She keeps saying, Samya, you can do this, and I have. I teach arts and crafts to little children who come here for day care.

Samya's account was echoed in the other discussions I had with the women of al-Hilal. They claim their activism has given them a new perspective. They sense a shifting framework of thinking, one that rises above the mundane, as evidenced in Samya's account. Being involved in Islamic activism both reorients their daily lives and shifts their focus from repetitive household routines to a wider context that offers new meaning and purpose. Whereas in the past, Samya was overwhelmed with these tasks, they now have become not only more manageable but also part of her activism. Ensuring the health and well-being of her family is part of improving society.[9]

Samya's housework is now organized; her day is structured; her children are under control; and her life has a sense of purpose. These newly acquired practices, clearly part of the vision imparted by the *gam'iyah,* epitomize the secular liberal values of modernity that nation-state building processes are meant to instill in women as the guardian of the family and the symbol of the nation. Samya embodies what Doctora Zeinab described as a "whole person" in her account of the position of women in Egyptian society today.

Samya's organization of her day is only one aspect of al-Hilal's structured discipline, which I repeatedly observed in the ways time was accounted for. Productivity was measured in the kitchen and in the sunny workshop where women were taught how to produce arts and crafts to sell at the bazaar. But most important, productivity was part of the social transformation of a small village, twenty miles east of Cairo, where a subcommittee of al-Hilal women ran a large-scale development project, which I describe in chapter 6.

Not all the women at al-Hilal were housewives; some of them held jobs in either the private sector, working in hotels and businesses, or in the public sector, medical labs, and government offices. Each of the women activists provided a valuable contribution to her community, whether it was her skills, talents, or work background.

Continuity and Disjuncture: Stories of Self/Subject

The narratives of the women describing the history of their engagement with Islamic movements are like modern-day dramas. These stories of self-transformation have a coherent logic and apply a bounded structure to messier realities. Ethnographies detail these projects, which Lene Rasmussen (2004, 71) calls "narratives of conversion." Tracing an explicit departure from a secular, material self to a religious and ethical ideal, women participants in Islamic movements almost always see themselves as departing from a superficial and unproductive way of life to one in which they recognize their self-worth as knowledgeable believers and active members of their societies. Wilhelmina Jansen (1998), who studied women in Islamic movements in Algeria and Jordan, affirmed the thematic sequence of these accounts, pointing out the departure and arrival in which the secular is juxtaposed with the Islamic.

While some of the women I talked with emphasized the strong religious force that pulled them toward Islamic activism, almost all described their lives before that as not having been particularly pious. Women construct these stories as journeys derived from a loss of direction. After much deliberation and self-searching, activist women begin with a first step. Dalia, an Islamic activist at al-Hilal, remembered that even after going on a pilgrimage to Mecca, often an experience that ends in deciding to wear the veil or *hijab*, she was not motivated in that regard:

> When I came back from the *haj*,[10] I was not wearing the *hijab*. I just did not think that was something I was ready for. It did not seem at all relevant to the feelings I had inside. I think the phenomenon of the *hijab* is unhealthy, because it needs to come out of certain behaviors. The word *muhajabbah*,[11] or *hijab*, is not in our religion. As a religion, Islam is quite lenient. It is a religion that values women.

Then Dalia stated in English, "You feel like a . . . a . . . princess" (she tried searching for a better word, gave up, and then shrugged her shoulders). She continued in Arabic:

> Our next-door neighbor while I was growing up was a pious woman. My parents often let me go there to play with her children. She was the one who taught me how to pray when I was seven. Then later, I watched this film on TV, *Rab'a al-'Adawiyya*; it just transformed me. I was taken by the powerful message in the film. The love of God is so great that you can transcend all the indignities of life, in the way that Rab'a was able to remain unaffected by the torture and abuse where the nonbelievers kept her. She had a saying that remained etched in my brain: *Law ana taliba jannatic la to'tiniha wa in kont kha'ffah min narrak faihriqny biha. Inama uhibaka lithatak.*

[If I were asking for your heaven, do not give it to me, and if I were afraid of your hell (lit. fire), burn me with it. But I love you (only) for your self].

I listened to Dalia talk about love for God as she explained it further using a quotation that she attributed to Sufists: "Sufists have an interesting saying that I like to think of when I am working. They say, '*Law 'alim ma nahn fih min mot'at al-'ibadah lanaza'na 'alayha milouk al-ard bil suyyuffi*' [If the kings of the earth knew of the pleasure we derive from worship, they would fight us for it with swords].[12]

Although not a Sufi herself, Dalia drew on the Sufi tradition's emphasis on the love of God and the mystical union with the divine. She was describing a long journey, one that began at the age of seven when she used to visit her pious neighbor who told her stories about the history of Islam and Islamic heroes. Her greatest inspiration, however, came from the 1950s film about one of Islam's most notable Muslim women, Rab'a al-'adawiyya, a celebrated medieval Sufi mystic. She saw in Rab'a the Muslim ideal that guided her own self-image as a Muslim woman. Yet it was clear that she did not consistently follow Rab'a's example. Dalia mentioned to me on another occasion when we were discussing her activism that she had worked at the Marriot hotel and was doing quite well in sales, where the products that she was selling were the pursuit of leisure and pleasure:

I do not do what I do [i.e., Dalia was in charge of both arts and crafts education for women and the store that sold their products] because I ask forgiveness or a reward from God. Nor am I motivated by a need to invest my energy in something useful. You know, I was once a top executive at the Marriott hotel. I was so good at my job in the sales department that I was awarded a Best Employee certificate. What I do, I do out of love for God.

Dalia's career at the Marriott began after she had seen the film and was inspired by its message. In her story, she does not mention this period in her life when she was not as pious as she would have liked, or the contradictions between her materialist desires and ambitions for a job, or that perhaps she turned to religious activism for other reasons.

She does not speak of moments when she might have questioned her decisions. Her story is only about finding Islam.

Dalia's journey was reproduced in many other narratives I heard, modern narratives of conversion or self-transformations revolving around bounded notions of selfhood and linear ideologies of change. Consider this passage from *Wagh bila makyaj* (*A Face without Makeup*) (1994), by Mona Yunis, an Islamic activist-writer, which describes the subject's "arrival" at the Islamic goals of becoming:

> These days were the best of my life. I realized that Islam is not just to perform prayer, to fast, to pay alms, and to go on pilgrimage. It is much more comprehensive and more general. I understood as well, that the *hijab* is just one step on the right path, and that this step has to be followed by other steps. I realized that a lot of women are satisfied by this first step, as if it were a goal in itself. We felt responsible, so we practiced *da'wa*. (Yunis 1994, 93–94, quoted in Rasmussen 2004, 74)

Yunis's story and countless others I have heard are personal sagas of self-discovery and *hidaya*.[13] What is interesting about this quotation, and commonly expressed by other activists, is the clear distinction between practices, such as wearing the veil, that are purely superficial for some when perceived as a goal in itself and the active pursuit of *da'wa*, which calls for raising the social awareness of Islamic teaching and ideals, as a social responsibility for others and for society. The drive and motivation to translate faith into practice are apparent, and the pursuit of *da'wa* is a demonstration of the deepest faith. With the ultimate goal of gaining closeness to their God, thousands of women in Egypt today similarly devote themselves to various causes across the country that are organized and funded by women. I believe that these Islamic endeavors are imbricated with the secular nationalist process of subject production informed by postcolonialist agendas of modernity. An examination of the processes that inform and produce these women's subjectivities cannot ignore the importance of these modernizing forces, which merge with religious elements.

In my interviews with many of the women participating in the Islamic movement in Cairo, I observed that they felt a need to verbalize the story of their engagement with Islamism. I realized that these stories about piety are central to their mission of *da'wa*, or spreading the word of Islam. They define and redefine their desires and subjectivities[14] in these stories so as to construct a homogenous process of self-fashioning and identity making, which Katherine Ewing labeled the "illusion of wholeness" (1997). The "stories" they told did not speak of transitions or processes but described their "before" and "after" conditions of self-hood. More often than not, the stories represented their original self as motivated by secular, modern, and materialistic desires that they reified as the binary opposite of their newly acquired religious self. Described as lost, this secular self was replaced by a new and improved religious self that usually, for no reason other than being in the right place at the right time, enters the world of Islamism and therefore is redeemed and improved through religious enlightenment and involvement in the movement. This theme in conversion narratives demonstrates that this new Islamic subject finds life less conflictual than before and that things make sense and enable the subject to perform one's social duties much more efficiently and successfully than before.

The self is described as an autonomous, bounded self in search of expression and realization. The experience of conversion, although a long process, is often collapsed into a definable period. But more important, the transformation from secular to religious self is presented as a complete and coherent process. Conversion narratives leave out any interruptions, trajectories, and disruptions.

These narratives of conversion are not just a celebration of religious zeal but are testimonials to the clear distinctions that to Islamic women activists, they must make between secularism and religion. In turn, these distinctions reflect the modernizing, nationalizing, secular discourse of the state. While simultaneously referring to the relevance of religion to all aspects of life and the spiritual nature of Islam that permeates all daily activities, the Islamic women activists I talked with consistently made references congruent with the nationalist motto *Al-din lil lah wa'l wattan lil gami'* [Religion is for God, and the nation is for everyone].[15] Women activists sometimes deliberately evoke these demarcations between the political and the religious to avoid harassment from the state, although the assumptions separating the religious from the secular state's modernizing ideologies remain embedded in their discourse. Some observers see this as indicating the participants' unspoken political aims, even though these binary oppositional ide-ologies clearly shape the movements' trajectories. This does not mean that all Islamic movements in Egypt adhere to such principles, but it points to the specific context of women's movements in Cairo. There are no apparent contradictions in women's discourse regarding these distinctions. The same women who talk about once being secular and suddenly discovering religiosity, describing the two states as separate and bounded, also talk about religion as a personal experience that permeates all aspects of life and informs ways of being and becoming.

Although the women of al-Hilal conceded that they constantly had to question and renew their intentions for becoming activists, through a processes of *tajdid al-niyya* (renewing intentions), they were able to maintain a unified, pious self. Their narratives construct "an illusion of wholeness," a homogeneity that follows a narrative structure of becom-ing. Islamic women activists' dialogic production of selfhood, finite in their depictions, also reveals ambivalence, contradiction, and overlap in their desires. This was apparent in their discussions, behaviors, and views on life. They acknowledged that their desires were not always focused on pious goals, that desire could pull them in different ways, which showed their awareness of "being human." As they told and retold their stories, the women of al-Hilal pursued this "wholeness," honing their desire for piety and devotion to Islam as they constructed their subjectivities through discourse.

The women of al-Hilal described their activism—which combined *da'wa* (an invitation to Islam, or spreading the word of Islam) and social development—in terms emphasizing a desire to please their God and to be a productive member of the community. Their descriptions of activism varied in their illustrations of the extent to which seculariz-ing modernization schemes had affected the way they focused on their productivity as women, their primary emphasis on education, and the place of religion in the private domain. These are the values that cen-tury-long processes of modernization by the state sought to inculcate in citizens so as to become accountable, disciplined individuals.

When I asked Laila how she would compare the activism at al-Hilal with what the Rotary Club (originally a secular, British, international philanthropic organization with a large following among professional Egyptians), she replied:

It is clear that the Rotary Club does some excellent work. We, however, have a very different outlook, although we might have the same projects, such as helping the poor and the needy. In our case, our fund-raising, for instance, would never plan a black-and-white party or a pop concert to raise money. Our ways are different. Our fund-raising is carried out under an Islamic umbrella, which means that we need to be true to our religion and our hearts. Our intentions and our aims are different, as we do not desire fame or recognition for our actions. Our biggest desire is God's blessing: *Wa qol 'immalo fa sayara Allah 'amalakom wa rassoulah wa'l mo'minoon* [Act so that Allah, his prophet, and believers will witness your work].

This work is based on each person's profession. It's like any other career. It is in my heart. It is a selfless and moral exchange. As a Muslim woman, I have a duty to improve the Muslim society I live in. How could it improve without an exchange between rich and poor, educated and uneducated, healthy and unhealthy?

So our duty extends to both Muslims and non-Muslims.

I don't care about nationalism. My driving force is my duty as a Muslim to give.

Laila's articulate response revealed a complexity and wide range of ideas. She is maintaining that Islamic activism is "like a career" but is in her heart and that although religiously motivated, this activism is an exchange through which society can improve. To Laila, the quality of activism distinguishing it from any other work is its relationship to God. This relationship gives her activism a frame of reference different from that of other kinds of activism. Her value system, for instance, does not emphasize good deeds or need public recognition.

Nationalism is not Laila's principal desire. Although she identifies herself as an Egyptian citizen, Laila defines herself first as a Muslim woman. She is not particularly concerned with the "state," and although she often talks about the corruption of the government and the lack of an effective agenda to address people's needs, Laila stays away from politics because to her, politics are not relevant to her activism. The actions, behaviors, and practices of Islamic women engaged in these movements are the product of a relationship with the divine. This bond runs very deep, which almost everyone I talked to at al-Hilal mentioned as particularly important to her. "I am like a devoted wife to God," Laila observed.

At the village of Mehmeit, Amal, an al-Hilal activist, was addressing a group of carpet weavers at the workshop that she started in the village to allow the younger women to earn some extra money. Her words of advice resonated with what I had heard in the religious lessons and discussions: "If everything you do everyday, you do with him [Allah] in mind, you will be able to reach a high level of perfection in your work. You must remember that all your actions are seen by Rabinah [our God]. When you do, you will do a better job and be successful in your life."

Al-Hilal's work ethic is summarized as follows in Amal's words:

Whether, they pray, teach, or embroider; make baskets, cook, or weave beautiful oriental rugs, their motivating factor is always the desire to please their creator, that the memory of him is motivation, and that his surveillance of their actions is enough deterrent from less than perfect work.

Their desire to be closer to God was paramount to them. The activists at al-Hilal improved themselves through *tajdid al-niyya*, or the renewal of intention, which is a process of self-reflection that enabled them to pause and question their motives in order to ensure that their desires were focused only on the pursuit of piety. The process of renewing their intentions was not prohibitive or punitive; it was an acknowledgment of the temporality of human desire.

Islamic women activists described their desires in terms that expressed their understanding of religion and reflected their belief that as a group, they could help transform the lives of people in need. By seeing their individual desires as personal, they separate the public and the private spheres of their modern selves. These demarcations mirror the state's modern secular ideals that it hoped to instill in the Egyptian population. As scholars have shown, modernization projects are intended to transform the position of Islam from practices permeating social and political life, to what secular liberalism defined as a religion. By religion, I mean the bounded category in Western thought, which is redefined and regulated by the state to diminish its role in politics and governance as well as to simultaneously serve state interests. These secular ideals cannot be realized, however, without reconfiguring the individual into a bounded and autonomous citizen of the state. In so doing, social space is divided into private and public, with religious practice largely confined to the private sphere.

In the Islamic women activists' discourse, Islam as a religion, as a way of life, and as a personal relationship with the divine is a naturalization of the personal and private aspects of religion. Such views are not perceived as contradictory. In a discussion with Samya, with whom I had many conversations regarding the disciplinary aspects of activism, I decided to push our conversation a little further. "How can Islam be a way of life and not a government?" I asked. This was her response:

> I don't govern anything but my own life.
>
> Islam is particularly attentive to the issue of *la darar wala dirar*, meaning that you do not have to follow an Islamic practice that causes harm to you or hurts you in any way.[16] For example, Qur'an prohibits the consumption of pork, but in a time of famine if the only food available is pork, then you are allowed to eat it. Necessity for survival can sometimes justify suspending a practice like wearing the veil in the United States after September 11. Muslim women were advised to stop wearing the veil in places where it might endanger their life. In some circumstances, however, this is not applicable. According to the rule of *la darar wala dirar*, in Egypt in the absence of Islamic law, as Muslims we need to apply the rule in instances when our Islamic obligations and rights are not being taken into consideration.

Although many Islamic women were in favor of an Islamized social life in Egypt, in which Egyptians' behavior and ethics followed Islamic principles, they were ambivalent about the establishment of an Islamic state. Some of them, like Laila, were resigned to the fact that Egypt would never become an Islamic state and hence questioned the point of pursuing the issue. They all, however, were against the idea of imposing an Islamic state on anyone. This is what I discovered in a conversation I had with Malak about the establishment of an Islamic state in Egypt:

If what you mean by an Islamic state is that you would force people to follow an Islamic system, then, no, I am not in favor of an Islamic state in Egypt. We do not have that kind of goal at heart.

Don't think I am passive, but we don't believe in force.

We have a huge percentage of women who come to al-Hilal. I help them learn how to read and write. I am ready to help them learn. But I do not force them: *Mabaslibsh iraditha* [I do not rob her of her will].

Take, for example, Saudi Arabia. It is a *salafi* society.[17] Islamic law is applied 100 percent in Saudi Arabia, but in their daily lives [the people] are not Islamic, for example, in their treatment of women. It is very common for Saudi Arabian men to marry as many as four wives, and they do not treat them equally, nor do they give women their rights according to Islam.

Our legal codes in Egypt are based on the Napoleonic codes. Does this mean we are French? No it does not.

Malak's views of an Islamic state have a number of interesting points. The demand by various Islamic groups for an Islamic state in Egypt has been expressed publicly in the past by the influential Muslim Brotherhood, and it has escalated the issue by insisting on participating in national elections. But because it is secular, the Egyptian government prohibits the establishment of political parties with religious affiliations, which automatically excludes the Brotherhood's demands. Today, the Muslim Brotherhood states very clearly that it does not pursue an Islamic state, since, according to them, they control the Egyptian street.

The women of al-Hilal, however, have a different Islamist desire for an Islamic state. In Malak's words, "force" is what she opposes. At the core of Malak's objection to the idea of an Islamic state is "the lack of choice" afforded to people. Her example of an illiterate woman who does not have the ability to choose is interesting. Opponents of democracy in Egypt claim (as did the British colonialist power in response to nationalist demands for independence) that the lack of education and illiteracy of almost half the Egyptian population denies them the right to democracy. But Malak insists on women's right to choose, that as an educated woman, she has no right to rob that of another woman. The liberal undertones in her emphasis on choice, her rejection of the idea of an imposed Islamic state, and her views on the Islamic rights denied women in Saudi Arabia show that the goals of modernizing projects that emphasize choice, individuality, voice, and independence match her Islamic ideals.

We cannot assume, however, that these values can be directly attributed to liberal modernity alone and not to Islamic teachings, or vice versa. As I illustrated in the last chapter, the history of mutual relations that imbricate human subjectivity makes it inaccurate to separate out liberal or Islamic values in discourse. Emphasis on the source or origin of these values is ultimately not of concern to us here. Historically, however, we can infer that these imbricated values become inculcated in people to varying degrees, by means of the state's disciplinary institutions.

The most significant point in Malak's account, however, lies in her claim that legal codes do not form a culture. An Islamic state does not necessarily produce an Islamic way of life, and as she mentions, the fact that Egypt follows legal codes that in principle are based on the Napoleonic codes does not necessarily produce a French population. This is important because it reflects a clearly secular ideal that separates the state's legal and political systems from the religious and cultural aspects of social life without seeing them as contradictory. In fact, Malak advocates a secular political system based on free choice and democracy rather than an Islamic state imposed involuntarily.

In this chapter, I examined women's Islamic activism at *gam'iyat* al-Hilal through the accounts of the women activists and the stories they told about the history of al-Hilal and the values and principles on which they base their Islamic teaching and activism. Their accounts made apparent that they defined their activism in terms of love of God and dedication to the word of Islam. Their desire is to please him and to ensure that they each perform—to the best of their ability—their Islamic duties. Social activism is an expression of this religious duty, according to these women. They see themselves in light of an Islamic ethic that binds them to extend their services to those in need.

These Islamic women talked freely about their activism. They were proud of their collective achievements and of al-Hilal as an instrument of Islamic reform. As they spoke about their love for God and their commitment to Islam, they simultaneously rejected the imposition of an Islamic state on the Egyptian population. To Malak, who expressed this sentiment, this was tantamount to "stealing the will of the people" and unacceptable, since the women of al-Hilal believe that there is no forcing in Islam. Their criteria for leadership were emphasis on Islamic knowledge, dedication, and commitment to activism, within the disciplinary ethos of liberal secular projects of modernization. These criteria were exemplified in their emphasis on education as a distinguishing factor and on the ability to think critically and acquire knowledge. Excellence was central to a leader, not merely knowledge but also organization and punctuality.

The women of al-Hilal emphasized these secular liberal values in their normalization of religion as a private experience. Seeing Islam as a private relationship with God but not as a public state system contradicts some of their claims that Islam is a way of life and even the dogma of prominent Islamic groups in the country that are actively pursuing the idea of an Islamic state. But the assumption that religion is private echoes the liberal secular basis of modern thought seeking the marginalization of religion to the private sphere as an essential step to social control and discipline of the individual. The fact that Islamic activists' discourse subscribes to these principles attests to the imbrication of liberal secular values in their own subjectivities and desires. In turn, this underscores the need for theory to move beyond normative depictions of "religious subjectivity" and emphasis on unitary religious subjectivity.

Although informal to some degree, the administrative system at al-Hilal paid special attention to productivity and scheduling. The values of organization, punctuality, and productivity could be found in stories told about domestic work, as in Samya's account. She observed that after becoming part of al-Hilal, she had been able to better organize her chores at home and to teach her children the values of free choice and independence. These are some of the subtle ways that the women of al-Hilal express the disciplinary principles of modern liberal thought. Others, like Laila and Malak, mentioned freedom, independence, productivity, and autonomy, which the women of al-Hilal expressed as important to women in society in general. The seamless ways by which they incorporated their ideals into Islamic teachings reflect the public discourses of modernization and progress emerging from Egypt's specific history.

I explored the imbricated values of liberal modernity with Islamic principles at al-Hilal, examining the activists' practices and views of religion. The next chapter takes a closer look at the specific case studies of women at the *gam'iyah*. My main objective is to explore the women's processes of self-production by focusing on ideals of Muslim femininity. These cases closely follow the extent to which the concomitance of Islamic tradition and secularism are embedded in their discourses and practices.

5

Desires for Ideal Womanhood

Throughout my conversations, interviews, and discussions with the activist women of the *gam'iyat* al-Hilal, I discerned slippages in their accounts, revealing both secularist and Islamic principles. Often these were clear-cut, such as the way that they seemed to have difficulty describing what *din*, or religion, meant to them—because it was so normative—and then they would say that it was about "an internal, personal relationship" between them and God or, very commonly, that "it was a way of life." Perhaps one of the most salient examples comes from the women who said that what motivated them to become pious was their religious education at school or a film they watched on television as a child.

The general view of the domestic as separate from the public was another assumption underlying their discussions, although their activism permeated these constructs. Secularist principles inculcated through modernization projects propagated by the state through public institutions, such as education, the media, and television, merge with Islamic ideals that activist women selected and propagated through religious lessons and activism. These fragmentary pieces making up the "illusion of wholeness" were fascinating examples of subjectivity shaped by contradictory and changing discourses of power. As I pointed out in chapter 3, histories of conflicting state agendas, colonialism, and Islamization contextualize subject-making processes. Next I consider how individuals in a community of pious activists paint portraits of themselves and how the ethnographic method can interpret their images.

Rhizomatic, Multiple, and Seamless Desiring Subjects

How do we account for these individuals and communities who seamlessly transcend binaries? Are we destined to remain within the confines of one or another particular theory? Should we not persist in searching for adequate ways to understand the processes mediating the desires of postmodern subjects? My intention was not to search for hybrids with histories of preconceived elements but to think of subjectivities as flows, changing in various uncharted ways. The analytical approaches and methodological processes that informed my research data avoided tracing liberal, as opposed to nonliberal, elements. Doing so would have risked essentializing the qualities of the "liberal modern" and the "Islamic traditional" as oppositional others, thereby reifying new binary constructs. Gilles Deleuze and Félix Guattari's (2004) idea of the rhizome is a useful metaphor of the unbounded versus the bounded. A *rhizome* refers to connections between points that may or may not be linked to the same nature. Most important, it refers to directions in motion and therefore escapes linearity. The rhizome is useful for examining the discourse of women who engage with Islamic activism, since the idea of flows offers more ways in which we may view Islamic women as multiple subjects with diverse and rhizomatic desires. Because women's engagement with Islamic teaching links them to the realm of "religion," their stories contain analytical binaries, whether or not they are represented as libratory subjects. They are either resistant to patriarchy or they embrace subjection. These theoretical postulations fail to open a discursive space that accounts for the women who may engage in pious activities and self-amelioration but who rhizomatically adopt liberal secular values. As Deleuze and Guattari point out, "The notion of unity (*unité*) appears only when there is a power takeover in the multiplicity by the signifier or a corresponding subjectification proceeding" (Deleuze and Guattari 2004, 9). The desires of these activist women continue to be shaped by power narratives that challenge their world and frame them as stakes in the power struggles of a century-long debate between religious groups and secular politicians.

In Western thought, the history of the self is often based on the traditional humanistic assumptions of Cartesian philosophy. Seen as a universal ingredient of human consciousness, the self is understood as the product of the division of mind and body, reason and nature. Attempts to critique the early Cartesian view of consciousness favored a perspective that equated the self with autonomous agency and viewed it as originating in the body (Merleau-Ponty 2002). While analyses of subjecthood were carried out in accordance with Western values of autonomy, freedom, and independence, current studies like Gloria Anzaldua's "Borderlands / La Frontera" critique the notion of the "unitary subject" and move beyond it to embrace the value of "living on the border." The complexity of Anzaldua's definition of herself as a Chicana, Mexican, lesbian, American, academic, writer, and activist is lived out in her not as a unitary subject but as multiple subjectivities. Anzaldua asks us to stay at the edge of what we know, to question our own epistemological certainties, and, through that risk and openness to another way of knowing and of living in the world, to expand our capacity to know the human. She believes that only through the mode of continuous translation can we produce a multifaceted understanding of multiplicity.

Subjects are formed through the intricacies of power relations (Deleuze 1988; Foucault 1979), but the focus of theorists of postmodernity is on interpreting how the subject represents itself, rather than the subject itself. Judith Butler (1993) argues that the subject is not an entity but is continuously shifting, fragmented, and performative. Deleuze and Guattari (1983) further challenge the notion of the subject by claiming that it is an unbounded and fluid series of flows. They reject the idea of a stable "I," or a fixed core, and the notion of a fixed subject position. They assert that postmodern subjects are schizophrenic desiring beings and call for the elimination of the ego altogether in favor of an unregulating, desiring unconscious. To them, the subject is not an entity or fixed but may be understood as rhizomatic.

A rhizome is an organism without a center that spreads continuously without beginning or end. Deleuze and Guattari use the concept of the rhizome to challenge humanist thought, which they describe as a "tree." To them, Western humanist thought is arborescent and ordered, since it is based on the assumption of an origin, or a totalizing structure, and continues according to a plan. To view the subject as unitary or as belonging to one nature is to ignore the rhizomatic multiplicities of subjecthood and the complex multiplicity of subjectification among the women activists I came to know at *gam'iyat* al-Hilal. The concept of the rhizomatic subject enabled me to see and appreciate the contradictions and inconsistencies in their discourse and to realize that their desires could not be described as nonliberal or have a definable essence or core.

The concept of a rhizomatic subject thus defies the notion of a "hybrid." In a debate with José Casanova over whether the presence of religion in the public sphere threatens the tenets of modernity, Talal Asad contended that the sanctioned role of religious groups in politics results in the creation of modern "hybrids" (2003, 182):

> For when it is proposed that religion can play a positive role in modern society, it is not intended that this apply to any religion whatever, but only to those religions that are able and willing to enter the public sphere for the purpose of rational debate with opponents who are to be persuaded rather than coerced. Only religions that have accepted the assumptions of liberal discourse are being commended, in which tolerance is sought on the basis of a distinctive relation between law and morality. (2003, 183)

Asad's analysis is helpful in understanding groups like al-Hilal. They maintain a sanctioned space for themselves precisely because their participants intentionally or unintentionally adopt liberal values. Asad views these groups that negotiate and adapt to secular norms as hybrids. Although the discourses of the Islamic women activists I worked with embed both liberal and Islamic concepts, these discourses have not evolved as hybrids. The main reason is the limitations in using the concept of hybrids, which are problematically viewed in postcolonialist literature as "the creation of new transcultural forms within the contact zone produced by colonization" (Ashcroft, Griffiths, and Tiffin 2003, 118). H. K. Bhabha (1996) called this the "Third Space," suggesting that cultural systems and conceptual productions are created through the interconnectedness of colonizer and colonized. This perspective, although it challenges binary thinking, implies that there are essential concepts to begin with that are later hybridized. Asad's use of hybridity in his view of the secular public space and the role of Islamic groups in it is problematic in that it implies that the secular space and religious groups originally possessed elements that later were hybridized when these religious groups entered the public sphere.

In this chapter I present a number of case studies of women activists at al-Hilal in order to explore theese nuances in their desires and subjectivities on a more personal level. In selecting these case studies, I tried to bring to the ethnographic data a diversity of backgrounds in education, socioeconomic levels, and age group.

Doctora Zeinab

Now in her early fifties, Doctora Zeinab is a retired physician who commands great respect and admiration from the women of al-Hilal, who regard her as a role model. From their accounts and my meetings with Doctora Zeinab myself, I see her as a highly regarded leader of the center of al-Hilal but also as a *da'iyah*, an example of the dedicated and hardworking Islamic woman activist. Another activist, Dina, described Doctora Zeinab as follows:

> She is just an amazing woman. You know, she is a medical doctor. Her husband is also an accomplished neurosurgeon. Yet despite her social standing, I saw Doctora Zeinab cleaning the toilets by herself right before one of our charity bazaars. When one of the other women suggested that she call one of the janitors, Doctora Zeinab said, Please don't keep me from earning good deeds from God. You see how modest she is?

Doctora Zeinab's modest and unassuming manner do not, however, undermine her leadership qualities that, as the head of al-Hilal, require that she be firm, assertive, and demanding of her community of activists. Even though Doctora Zeinab is the center's main decision maker, she projects a sense of camaraderie and warmth that is impossible to miss. She sees her main goal as "bringing out the good in people." Laila, who works at al-Hilal, told me,

> I have been attending Doctora Zeinab's religious sessions since 1991, and I find her an open-minded person, worthy of respect. Her

knowledge of Islamic theology and teachings are outstanding. When there is something she is not sure about, she admits it and doesn't avoid the subject. She spends most of her time discussing behavior, a practice she finds more important than reading the Qur'an for the fifteenth time.

Doctora Zeinab is the mother of three children, two boys who now have families of their own, and a daughter, who was especially close to her and also involved in Islamic activism but died in 2006 of cancer. Although Doctora Zeinab suffered in dealing with her daughter's illness and then death, she never stopped going to the *gam'iyah*, despite the time she spent with her daughter at the hospital. On the day her daughter died, she telephoned Laila with the sad news. But that was not the main purpose of her call; she asked Laila to visit one of the women who volunteered at the center who had just had a hysterectomy. She apologized for asking her to go in her place but explained that it was too difficult for her to go to a hospital again so soon after her daughter died. Laila understood and relayed Doctora Zeinab's regrets to the patient. Laila remarked that although Doctora Zeinab was very composed, her vulnerability at these moments demonstrated her belief that for humans, pain and anguish are a part of life that must be experienced. Her activism helped her to pull through this tough time and provided her with the support of the women with whom she shared so much.

Islam views death as God's will and not a tragedy. To Muslims, death is merely a journey, and they are encouraged to get on with their lives because grieving excessively is considered un-Islamic. Islam also prohibits wailing, beating the chest, and wearing mourning clothes. Wailing is not socially acceptable behavior in Egyptian society, as women in particular are seen to be lacking decorum if they succumb to what is perceived as an excessive display of emotion. Although mourners in Egypt are expected to wear black as a sign of mourning, emotional displays are generally associated with ignorance and misguided behavior. The Prophet Muhammad instructed Muslims to mourn for only a short period: "It is not lawful for a woman who believes in Allah and the day of judgment to be in mourning for any deceased person for more than three nights, except for her husband, for whom the period of mourning is four months and ten days."

The Islamic practice of mourning shows great variety from one location to another and from time to time. Societies in which the individual is at the center of social processes place a stronger emphasis on mourning and public demonstrations of grief. For example, according to a study by historians Peter Jupp and Clare Gittings (1999), mourning practices in England followed historical and cultural changes. One of the interesting points they make is that between 1760 and 1850, roughly the time of the Enlightenment, the belief in the need for progress to take the world beyond an irrational and superstitious past affected death and funerary rites in England. The church no longer controlled the final rituals before internment, which were replaced by secular burial rituals. More important was the reduction in significance of the last rites performed by religious clergy. This shift placed the mourners, rather than the mourned, at the center of funerary rites. The transformation of thought and feeling about death continued with the influence of Romanticism and Evangelicalism on reactions to and experiences with death. Besides the secularization of death, urbanization, class, and socioeconomic distinctions all affected the individual's experience with death and dying.

Mourning and celebrating death are approached differently in Egypt and vary across socioeconomic classes. In the past two decades, funerals have shifted from a celebration of mourning and loss to a renewal of ties to God and acceptance of his control over people's lives. In Egypt, funerals are scheduled after the burial (burials are generally a simple affair with only the immediate family attending) and are held after the sunset prayer, at either the deceased's home or a local mosque. Currently, more and more families hold funerals at mosques rather than their home because of the convenience, easier accessibility, and more space and also because mosques now provide more services to the community than in the past. Women pay their respects in a special hall that today most mosques offer to mourners, while male relatives of the deceased occupy the main prayer hall. Verses from the Qur'an, chosen to remind the attendants of the imminence of death and to follow Islamic teachings in preparation for judgment day, are recited through loud speakers.

Yet, twenty years ago, most funerals were an elaborate three-day affair commonly held at people's homes. Well-to-do families hired white-robed waiters, or *suffragis* in *galabiyyas*, to serve tea and unsweetened Turkish coffee to those paying their condolences, who were dressed entirely in back. Women often talked quietly among themselves while the Qur'an was recited in the background. After an appropriate period of time, some people would get up and, paying their respects, they would leave in the interval between the recital of verses. In the mosque, however, silence is required during the recital. The atmosphere is more somber, and the goings and comings of those paying their condolences are quiet, usually because the mourners do not remain as long in the mosque. Crying and extreme emotions are discouraged in the mosque, and today, religious lessons both console and warn family members and friends that their turn could be sooner rather than later and that they need to act fast to redeem themselves. Piety and almsgiving are stressed as methods of improving one's religious performance and gaining a favorable place in the divine's regard.

Doctora Zeinab had her daughter's funeral at a local mosque. Family and friends paid their respects to a devastated but composed mother. I am told that she did not shed a single tear and that she sat as poised as ever, smiling and greeting the hundreds of people who came to pay their respects.

As a young girl growing up in the less affluent part of the neighborhood, Doctora Zeinab attended an Arabic-language school where she perfected her language skills. She also took classes in Islamic religion at school, where government books were used. She learned verses from the Qur'an, studied *al-sira al-Nabawiyya* (the history of the life of the Prophet Muhammad), and increased her knowledge of Islam. She grieved and suffered over her daughter, but her feelings of anguish were nevertheless shaped by her understanding of Islamic practices and beliefs, and the liberal values embedded in her understanding of this tradition. Her reactions to death included getting on with her own life and duties and viewing loss and grief as part of life that should not be denied. As a modern activist Islamic woman, Doctora Zeinab's subjectivity is shaped by complex and imbricated processes of both Islamic historical traditions and liberal secular ideals and principles.

Doctora Zeinab was introduced to Islamic activism when she was a student at Cairo University's School of Medicine. Although she attended a few meetings run by the women in the various Islamic groups on campus, she was more interested in understanding "what Islam was really about." Through reading and listening to religious tapes, she found herself drawn to the subject more and more. Meanwhile she met her husband in one of her classes at the university. Soon after, they became engaged and then married. Doctora Zeinab quickly realized that her family demanded more attention than her studies. Although she managed to graduate, she lost interest in pursuing a career as a doctor, despite practicing medicine for a while. After a few years of juggling her work and her now growing family, she found her interests shifting again to her study of Islam. At the time, the Ministry of Religious Endowments welcomed women to study to be preachers, and Doctora Zeinab enrolled in the classes at the institute for *da'wa*.

With some knowledge of *fiqh*, *shari'a*, and Qur'anic studies, as well as a certificate allowing her to preach, Doctora Zeinab was now well positioned to advance her knowledge on her own. In the next two years, she read everything she could find about the writings of such famous scholars as al-Ghazali and al-Qaradawi. She began to realize that her friends were always consulting her on issues of religion and that she found satisfaction in explaining Islamic teachings and helping other women learn about Islam. It was during this time that she heard about Hagga Warda (who started the first women's Islamic organization in this network of PVOs) in the neighborhood of Heliopolis and decided to attend her religious lessons. There she met other women who also were learning about Islam. She also was influenced by Hagga Warda's style of preaching and teaching. A year later, Doctora Zeinab felt ready to start giving Islamic lessons herself.

Doctora Zeinab explained how her preaching made her the kind of person that she is:

I didn't know I had it in me. *Al-da'wa* requires a certain kind of person. It is not only about knowledge; it is also about how you relay this knowledge and how you leave people wanting more. It is not about fear; it is about love. When I realized that I was gaining more confidence and my friends were telling me that I was already engaged in *da'wa* because I answered their questions and helped them learn about how to get closer to God, I agreed to give lessons at the sports club.

Religion is behavior and is not just about knowledge. Because I teach about Islam, I can't act differently from what I preach. I realized that because I am a *da'iyah*, I refer to God in everything that I do. This is *tajdid al-niyya* [renewing intention]. You start shaping yourself. I am responsible to him for what I teach and the way I act. Everything in life is related to religion.

It has to do with always keeping your intentions at the center of your thinking. This is not an easy task. We can keep our thoughts focused on a particular task but being aware of *niyyitik (your intention)* requires you to be always asking yourself: What was behind my actions? What prompted me to say this? Think, question yourself, but remind yourself that renewing your intentions *(tajdid al niyya)* constantly is not meant as a punishment or even a burden. It is about acceptance as well. It is aout knowing when your limits are as a human and seeing them clearly. To deny these limitations is denying you are human. What's the point of being created human if we have no limitations and everybody's exactly like God wants them to be?

Referring to God in everything that she does is no simple task but a constant process of self-discipline. Doctora Zeinab understands that this discipline is not automatic, that it is grounded in her knowledge of her own limitations as she copes with the stresses of life. The challenge of this process is made manageable through an acceptance of these limitations, and the reward of calm and peace when she pursues her desire of making her God a frame of reference. Hence, desire is not merely a point in time or a thing to be gained. It is a continuous process, one that she calls *tajdid al-niyya*, renewing intentions.

The importance of *tajdid al-niyya* is that it enables Doctora Zeinab to live her life as always in a state of becoming and not a continuously uninterrupted process of perfection. By acknowledging her own limits as a human being, she can shape her desires in accordance with Islam, but always with reference to these limitations to the evolving conditions of life.

According to Doctora Zeinab, intention, or *al-niyya*,[1] is

the core, the underlying purpose in anything that we do. Sometimes things become like a routine. You need to stop and revisit why you are doing what you are doing. You ask yourself, Am I an activist for

God, or am I doing this because I have grown to like the prestige it gives me? Or because I am lonely and need something to keep me involved? These are not bad intentions, but in order to do things for God, *li waghi Allah*,[2] I need to be able to constantly sharpen my focus. For example, when I go out to the street to do *da'wa* or to visit those who are in need, I meet all kinds of people: those who are needy and others who are just rude or unkind. I find myself in situations that can easily anger or upset me. But I remind myself of my *niyya*, that this isn't about me. It is about God and about pleasing him that I do this. As the Prophet's *hadith* maintains, *Inma al-'mal bil niyyat wa li kol imri'in ma nawa*.[3]

The death of Doctora Zeinab's daughter must have been one such challenge, although she did not talk about it with me. According to Laila, it was a trying time for Doctora Zeinab, who, like the rest of the women in the *gam'iyah*, strives to refer everything to God while having to learn to cope with what life offers, including grief and suffering. Laila described Doctora Zeinab as "a person who is disciplined in her life, not too involved with herself, and embracing her society within the guidelines of Islam."

Kamla

Kamla is in her late thirties. She has a trim figure and dresses in smart clothes, with her hair always neatly tucked under a long veil folded back along the sides of her head and secured with pearl pins to keep it in place. She has a nice, open smile that flashed across her face as she talked. Kamla's parents were simple, modest people. Her father was a government official in the Ministry of Agriculture, and her mother was a housewife who did not finish school. Kamla grew up with three other brothers and sisters, all of whom graduated from university. Like Doctora Zeinab, Kamla attended an Arabic-language school in the neighborhood, from which she went on to study agriculture in college. While attending college, she married an engineering school university graduate who now works at an engineering firm. To Kamla, her family and her activism are the center of her life.

Kamla teaches in the arts and crafts program for young girls at the *gam'iyah*. She developed a curriculum for them, which the *gam'iyah* published in a book for instruction on the arts.

I explained to Kamla that I was interested in her views on religion and activism and what they mean to her. As with many others at the *gam'iyah*, she was willing to connect somehow, to share her story.

I asked Kamla what "religion" meant to her. For the first few minutes, she seemed to be struggling to find the words. She began by saying, "Religion to me is the way I act . . . how I think. It is hard to express myself exactly . . . hmm. . . . It is how you live your life. Everything I do, I do thinking about Islam." As we talked about her relationship to religion, I sensed that Kamla was struggling to define clearly what religion was to her. In her words, religion was just how you lived your life. It inspired her thinking and gave her guidance in everything she did. Soon after she began talking, however, Kamla began using "Islam" in lieu of "religion," and her words and expression became more animated: "Islam is about loving God in my heart. Islam teaches you everything . . . everything you need to know is in Islam. . . . Islam is about how you treat others. It is about how you translate your faith into action."

Kamla then launched into her story to illustrate how following the path of Islam and becoming an activist had changed her life for the better. She began a narrative that now seemed familiar to me. She told me that when she was first married, she was not veiled, that she wore all kinds of things (she swept her hand in the air as if to say that she dressed like me. I was wearing pants and a long jacket that reached to my knees). Then she said that she and her husband went to *'umra* (a short pilgrimage to Mecca) and that when she came back, she felt her life would take a different turn.

Up to that time, Kamla had never worked outside her home. But now she started to pay attention to the Islamic social work in her neighborhood. She began going to a mosque where a small group of women got together to help the poor. Soon she heard of *gam'iyat* al-Hilal and took classes in *fiqh*. She declared that a whole new world opened to her, that Rabinah[4] was opening roads for her to get to know him. Kamla told me this in a practiced voice like those of the many women I had talked to previously who used the same themes in constructing their Muslim selfhood. It was at this time that Kamla found her new identity as an Islamic activist.

She then told me that what she learned from Doctora Zeinab's classes on Islam helped her become a well-educated person. Even her husband eventually told her that he was proud of her work, although in the beginning, he was displeased that she was spending so much time away from home. He was so proud, explained Kamla, that he would boast of her piety and Islamic knowledge to his friends. Besides taking lessons, she was helping at the center by teaching arts and crafts to the girls. I asked how she found the time to do all that. Kamla laughed. She said that before she worked at the center, she was not as well organized. In fact, being part of the group of activist women at the center helped her put her life in perspective and taught her how to complete her chores and plan her day. As she recounted this, Kamla reminded me of what another activist, Samya, had earlier said about herself:

> When you follow Rabinah in your heart and you know what he wants and aspire to do it, everything falls into place. Your life, including your kids and your husband and your home, seem to fit together. Everything you do begins to take on a different meaning. Doing things right is a kind of worship that you do for God's sake.

The religious lessons that Kamla attended at al-Hilal had a profound impact on her life and how she saw herself and others. One of the important ways in which her outlook changed was the way she began to deal with her own children and issues of discipline. This is an example of the liberal principles of child rearing, which emphasize individualism, choice, and persuasion over the traditional patriarchal norms often ascribed to Islamic teaching.

Kamla explained how her involvement in Islamic social work affected the way she had raised her three children. Her oldest, a son, is now a ship captain; her older daughter is in university; and her younger daughter is in school. Kamla said that she raised her younger daughter in a completely different manner than she raised her other two children because of the Islamic lessons she attended at the center. "All those lessons and all the discussions made me realize that forcing children to be obedient doesn't work." In fact, she says that "the way you approach kids is very important. You should be more of a friend than a parent." Kamla knew that her children would never become good Muslims if she forced them into doing things, that convincing them was better. She says that in the past, she expected her children to obey her but after she started taking lessons in Islam, she learned that persuasion was a more effective tool. "Before," she said, " I just yelled and demanded that they obey me. Now I take the other route, the route to their minds." What happened if they disagreed with her? "Well, I still tried to convince them. It's difficult because of many things today like the media, television, videos, and the movies, all send conflicting messages to kids." Kamla was now convinced that the best way to be a parent was to invite her children to understand why certain things were acceptable and others were not. Whereas in the past her authority as a parent was all she could muster in a confrontation with her kids, she found her parenting more effective when she did not enforce her power of authority over them. Instead of demanding obedience, as her parents did with her, she now saw her role as that of a guide, to explain what was right and wrong and to ensure that her children did not lose their way. By pointing out what she saw as unacceptable ways for women to act in music videos, she was, as she saw it, teaching her children the values of Islam, not through prohibition, but in a way that invited them to love religion and not fear it.

Kamla ascribed her newfound parenting techniques to Islamic teachings. She raised her children as individuals who said what they thought and who understood what was right and wrong so they could choose freely. This was a clear departure from traditional patriarchal practices that require a parent to be an unrelenting authoritative figure that dictated and demanded obedience. Kamla did not see these "traditional" forms of child rearing as effective as the Islamic methods she learned at the center.

Islamic teaching emphasizes using mercy and love to raise children. The Prophet Muhammad urged his followers to teach their children archery and horseback riding so that they would have independent skills and be able fend for themselves and excel in physical activities. Individualism, freedom of choice, and persuasion appear to be the emphasis that modern, liberal methods of raising children advocate, here similarly practiced by the center and followed in children's classes during weekends and summer vacation. This is significant because it reveals how activist women's ideas and normative beliefs about raising children are shifting to accommodate new forms of child rearing while rejecting the more patriarchal ways of raising children. These new emphases do not contradict Islamic teachings, which also emphasize the intellect as a pathway for belief. Principles of individuality are central to the production of modern, autonomous subjects in liberal secular ideologies, and they defy notions of personhood, often thought to be more relational and connective in traditional Middle Eastern societies. Yet as we observe how these "new" forms—in which liberal views of child rearing merged with Islamic teachings—are defined as Islamic, it becomes apparent how difficult it is to separate what is truly Islamic from other traditions.

"Learning *fiqh* [jurisprudence] taught me many things that I was not aware of before, like what rituals to perform when your menstrual period is over and how you purify yourself," Kamla pointed out. She has taken many courses on *fiqh* and now is an authority for herself and other women in regard to praying, fasting, and performing the rituals and laws of Islam. Kamla described her activism as purely religious. She was not interested in politics. Her training and education had made her a better believer and hence a better wife, mother, and active member of her community. Is Kamla's piety as private and religious as she says it is? Even though she clearly distinguishes in her mind between religious and political, her project of self is socially and politically imbricated. Many of the women from the women's Islamic movement described similar sentiments. They seemed to clearly delineate their activities from political objectives or nationalist ideals while simultaneously asserting that Islam was a way of life permeating all aspects of living. They did not see this as contradictory, nor did they seem to find it particularly challenging that Islam could permeate all aspects of their life when they had to obey a law that was based on secularism.

Laila

I knew Laila as a friend from my college years, yet I came to know a very different side of her as part of al-Hilal. Laila attended the American University in Cairo, graduating at the top of her class and going on to work on her master's degree in economics. For a while, Laila worked as a teacher's assistant and then took a job at a well-known international bank in Cairo. In the mid-1980s, Laila married a broker at the bank. Her decision to begin wearing a veil came a few years later and was as a surprise to her family and friends, who were not, according to Laila, "religious in any way." Her mother's friends ridiculed her (according to Laila, they are very Westernized), as they saw her act of veiling as a social demotion. For Laila, this was a trying time, and she often felt close to tears as she listened to these women describe the veil in derogatory terms. Often she would find herself in a defensive position from which she would have to bow out gracefully, for many of those who debated the importance of veiling were not well read or familiar with the important writers on the subject. What infuriated Laila was that they often cited secular writers like Farag Foda, who she sayswere opposed to Islam.

For Laila, religion evokes two images:

It is inner peace and a way of life. It is inner peace because religion enables you to be in harmony with yourself and to put things in perspective. It also is a way of life because it provides the guidelines for everything, buying and selling, dealing with other people, organizing society . . . etc. The Qur'an complemented by *sunnah* [practices and teachings of the prophet] supports the notion of the modern Islamic state.

I am from an unreligious family. Nobody ever told me to pray or fast. Doesn't everyone have a gift for something? Mine is being pious since I was a little girl. I learned how to pray at school. I attended the French Sacred Heart School. I remember when the religion teacher brought a praying mat to class so she could teach us how to pray. She had us stand in a line, and one after another we learned to perform ablutions and then to pray.

I can't remember what made me start to pursue praying consistently. Once, one of my classmates in university gave me a tape with a recording of a religious sermon. I remember listening to the tape and feeling scared. But I do know this. I always had an awareness of God's presence in my life. But for a while I even fasted inconsistently. I grew up oblivious to the nuances between *dunya* and *din* (the material world and religion). I used to put on a bathing suit and spend all my time on the beach in Alexandria.[5]

Laila clearly articulated her desire for closeness to her God, a relationship she constantly evaluated. Her notion of Muslim womanhood is the product of that desire. As she learns more about Islam, she shapes her personhood according to what her religion expects from her. It is not merely perfecting the close ties she enjoys with the divine but is action as well. What Laila perceives as an internal emotion of love must be accompanied by a socially productive role, one firmly embedded in social realities and does not advocate seclusion or retreat from this world:

> Love for God is my desire. It is a goal I pursue. I refer to my conscience in all that I do.
>
> Life is just a phase. As a Muslim, I am required to enjoy my life. *Wal mal wa'l banun zinat al-hayaht 'l donaya* [a Qur'anic verse meaning that money and children are the decorations of life]. The greatest evidence for this is that according to Islamic law, if you have money, only 2.5 percent goes to the poor. The rest is for you to enjoy, unlike socialist and capitalist systems, which impose high taxes on income. Although enjoying life is a principle allowed by Islam, this is not my goal. Money doesn't make me a good person. A good person is someone who is ethically sound and feels for others, has empathy. Part of Islam is that you do not seclude yourself. We do not follow the principle of monasticism or Sufism, we urge the principle of being positive *actors* in society.
>
> In my opinion, a woman has a dual responsibility to her house and her society. The error made by some Muslim people is to see women in a very small fixed cell. This gives the wrong idea about women's role in society.
>
> The Muslim woman can be a positive member of her society. This is not the picture propagated in the Western media about Muslim women, shown in a black tent, following on foot while a man rides comfortably on a camel! But I am not as concerned about this image of women as I am with the image of Islam.
>
> When I decided to pursue Islamic activism, I could have chosen other careers. Instead I was pulled into this work by a desire to help the poor. My first experiences were in 1997 and 1998 to become actively involved in people's lives. I was involved in projects dealing

with cancer patients, lepers, and orphans; I was driven by a humanitarian point of view that embraces the doctrine of Islam.

The last sentence of Laila's account, that she was driven by "a humanitarian point of view" and her frustration with Muslim women's image on news networks, seems at first to fit with her desire of love of God and Islam. It also shows an awareness that accompanies the project of shaping herself as a Muslim woman. As an educated, upper-middle-class woman of independent means, Laila also is part of a world that does not take her Islamism lightly. Laila is concerned about how she is perceived as a Muslim woman by her mother's Westernized friends or the Western media. Although she maintains that she is concerned more about the image of Islam and less with the image of women, Laila's socioeconomic class has a negative view of her Islamic affiliations. Hence, besides being driven by love for her God and Islam, she is driven by an existential desire to prove herself as a humane, educated, and accomplished Muslim woman to those who associate being Islamic with lower-class, backward, and misogynist practices.

I was interested in finding out how Laila dealt with gender issues in her activism. Laila told me that at al-Hilal they need to be careful with the women who come to the center, because addressing gender equality may create conflict at home for these women.

> We are constantly working in various spheres at the center. We volunteer our time and our efforts in somewhat dangerous conditions. Because we are not protected by the state, we have to be very careful in what we teach many of the women who come to the center. We cannot, for example, tell women to assert themselves to their husbands because an angry husband might come to the center the next day and beat me up [she said laughing].

But angry husbands are not all the activist women worry about. Although they seem to view Islam as private and their activism as nonpolitical, they also are aware of a state that wants to maintain the status quo. In a candid moment, Laila revealed her frustration about that, although hers was not a view shared by the rest of the women I interviewed:

It's true we also have to be careful because any move we make that can be perceived as political by the government would shut us down. We are closely monitored to stay away from politics. We cannot advocate politically for some of our causes, such as building schools or hospitals, because we are in danger of crossing that line. We are tolerated as long as we remain "religious."

Nonetheless, the women at the center did have a legal status. Many of them are certified by Al-Azhar as *da'iyat*, and the center itself is registered with the Ministry of Social Affairs. But what Laila was referring to is that they were not supported by the state but were merely tolerated as long as they stayed within their religious bounds, did not discuss politics, or engage in political activities of any sort. The distinctions these women make between Islamic practice and politics are not always as clearly delineated, however, as they make claim to knowledge that is historically and discursively produced through nationalist, postcolonialist, and modernist discourse.

Hagga Afaf

I had heard many of the women talk with great respect about Hagga Afaf, one of the cofounders of the center. She was a self-made Islamic scholar who was perceived as intellectual and moderate. She was soft spoken and always articulate. Hagga Afaf was a *da'iyah*, which meant that she was trained to teaching Islam and was well versed in *fiqh* and *shari'a*. One important fact about Hagga Afaf is that when she was in her early sixties, she also was working on her master's degree in the history of Islam from Cairo University. She was a very pleasant person, and despite her reputation as a scholar, she was unassuming and made very little of the fact that she was considered the scholar in residence at al-Hilal. Her round face with a ready smile and a warm appeal instantly charmed you when meeting her.

I was helping Hagga Afaf reshelf some books she had been showing me in the reading corner attached to her workspace when she started talking, with some prompting on my part, about herself and her activism. She grew up in a middle-class family of seven siblings in a popular area of Cairo known as Shubra. Her father was a professor at the University of Minya in Upper Egypt. Her mother, who finished only elementary school before her family decided to keep her at home to help her mother, had to take care of the entire family. Hagga Afaf remembers that her mother worked hard and never complained. "My mother was a very strong woman. She knew where each one of us was at all times. Despite her lack of education, she was very wise and intelligent and always offered good advice." Education was valued in this family, and Hagga Afaf's father insisted that she and her two sisters finish college before they got married.

When she was growing up in the 1950s, the new nation-state made education free for all, and her father, struggling to pay all their expenses, took advantage of that opportunity. At school, Hagga Afaf remembers the lines in the morning saluting the flag and singing the national anthem. "Those were times that made you proud to be an Egyptian. We felt like the chosen generation. Nasser was our hope. [But] the defeat in the 1967 war and his death a few years later buried our dreams. Egypt was never the same after that." In the early 1980s, her husband, who was a faculty member at Tanta University, applied for leave to teach in Saudi Arabia. It was an opportunity for them to save for their children's future. Hagga Afaf soon made a circle of friends in Jidda. They all were university wives from various parts of the governorates. She learned from them how to conduct herself in Saudi culture, which was different from her own. They all lived in the same neighborhood and would get together to perform the daily prayers, especially the al-'ishaa prayer at the end of the day. The men would sit in a circle discussing their day, and the women would often talk about shopping and instruct one another in religious rituals.

Knowledge, not only of Islam but also of other religions, is very important to Hagga Afaf. She recalled that when she came back from Saudi Arabia, her children, now college age, knew little about Egypt's history. So she decided to organize a series of trips to teach them their cultural heritage. She rented a bus with a few friends who also brought their children, and they took the group on tours of Cairo. They visited the Citadel of Salah al-Din and the Mosque of Mohamed Ali. They saw the hanging church of Old Cairo and got a special permit to visit the synagogue in Maadi. It was a wonderful experience, Hagga Afaf told me, one of the most memorable times with her children. Her sense of

initiative and concern for education went beyond teaching her children and the children of the neighborhood.

Education and knowledge are al-Hilal's greatest concerns. The
women there try to supplement the government school curriculum,
which they regard as stagnant and inept. Modernization schemes in
Egypt have generally placed the education of the population at the center of their projects. As a consequence, education has become a social
marker of prestige and a necessary vehicle for social mobility in Egyptian society. As studies have shown, Islamic intellectuals also enjoy a
revered position in society because of their knowledge of Islam (Eickelman 1985). The women at the *gam'iyah* mirrored a concern with both
general knowledge as well as Islamic teachings, and they go to great
lengths to develop curricula for children's after-school activities and
summer classes, which are revised every six months. Women activists
rely on documents (some of which are as long as 150 pages) for each
level to guide their classes. Because Hagga Afaf is the supervisor of the
educational program, she has a lot of responsibility, and her religious
tolerance and religious heritage are reflected in some of the students'
projects.

Her governing logic regarding religion and Islam is evident in the
following quotation:

> I believe there is a God for everyone, but it is the same God. Chris-
> tianity, Judaism, and Islam, all these religions share the same God. It
> is only politics that create the differences among them. There is one
> God and one religion; it doesn't matter which or which prophet or
> any of that. In the end, we all want the same thing, peace.

I asked Hagga Afaf to describe what she meant by religion. Her
reply was succinct: "Religion is the relationship of the individual with
his or her community and god," thus placing religion in the domain of
both the individual and the social. This is an important variation on
how religion is understood by the other members of al-Hilal. Using the
community to define the position of Islam in society is an approach
often taken by Islamic liberals. The writing of Mohamed Imara points
to the importance of the civic community in establishing an Islamic
way of life (as opposed to the more radical Islamist view maintaining

that *la hukma illa lilah,* that sovereignty belongs to God alone, thus enforcing the idea of an Islamic state. Imara contends that according to Islamic texts, the state's authority is derived from civil sources. Therefore it is the community that is entrusted with choosing a ruler and determining the ruler's efficacy. If the rulers fail to uphold Islamic law, the *Umma* has the right to depose them. According to Imara, this principle governs the role of religion in the state. Muslims already have a fair and just system that does not necessitate borrowing from the West (Imara 1991). But Hagga Afaf did not agree with Imara. She shook her head to my question about whether she envisions that road to the Islamization of Egypt: "Not at all. I do not mean it in that sense. I think that the community is important because it would not exist without the individual, and vice versa." Apolitical, private, and restricted to the individual and community, Hagga Afaf's interpretation of religion neatly parallels Egypt's nationalist secular discourse, based on liberal, modern, secular ideals separating religion from public forms of politics.

Salwa

Growing up in an upper-middle-class family in Egypt allows girls access to privileges such as a private school education and the opportunity for a university education. Salwa attended what was once a French missionary school. By the time she was a student there, however, after the 1952 revolution, its curriculum and teaching staff had begun to follow the Ministry of Education's guidelines, as was common in most of the European schools after independence. Although the school continued to be a "French"-language school and taught French as its main language, the teachers were no longer French, and Egyptian teachers were hired in their place. As did many of the graduates of French schools in Egypt, Salwa graduated with fluency in both French and English, as well as with a good command of Arabic.

Salwa attended the American University in Cairo, where she studied political science. While there, she did charity work with the Rotary Inner Wheel, a secular, international, elite philanthropic organization. She became more and more interested in social work and worked hard to develop various projects. But in her own words,

There was something missing there. I somehow did not feel entirely satisfied with what I was doing. It was only when I got more interested in Islamic classes that I realized that I was discovering a part of myself that I had been searching for. When I joined al-Hilal, I was already veiled and had quite a good background in *fiqh*. I nevertheless took more classes, and as I got more involved, I found myself looking for something more than just knowledge. It was then that I drew on my background in philanthropy from the Rotary to start doing social work here. Mehmeit came later. I got together with others who were looking to get involved in something bigger than just distributing donations and things like that. We wanted a more sustainable project that would help people live better lives in their own homes. We talked to a group of people at the Misr al-Gadida branch, and they invited us to visit one of their projects in the villages. We volunteered there for a while and helped them set up a literacy center in a poor village near Cairo. After that, Amal and I visited several villages until we decided on Mehmeit.

Salwa's daughter, who is fourteen, attends a private school in Cairo. Salwa noted that the Islamic way of raising her children had influenced her daughter, who has developed the habit of setting aside money to help the poor and joins Salwa on many of her trips to rural areas. Like many other teenagers her age, Ghada is involved in sports and is the captain of her volleyball team. She also is a swimmer and competes nationally with the sports club where she trains. I found it interesting that at her age, Ghada would be interested in spending her weekends in villages helping her mother. She admitted with a grin, "Sometimes I bring my iPod along and listen to music when I'm tired. It can be hard work, but I think it's fun."

About religion, Salwa observed,

To me, religion is intertwined with everything, only because it is an agenda for life, like a blueprint showing you the best ways to live. Religion enables us at the end of the day to rise above the mundane, the useless things that occupy a large portion of our waking hours, only to be forgotten when more serious things take their place. [Religion is] having a place to go to when all else fails.

Once again, the definition of Islam as an internal process provides a frame of reference for behavior or sanctuary from daily life.

> You just cannot cope with life today with all its challenges and temptations without having a religious background. Without religion, how can I raise my children, or how can I provide them with moral principles that can help teach them right from wrong? That would be a daunting task.

It seems clear that Salwa regards the internal private world of Islam as a frame of reference that does not take precedence over other goals. She made no mention of politics or political activism, although as the next chapter shows, the social transformation of villages such as Mehmeit might cause state officials some discomfort.

The case studies discussed here shed some light on the desires and subjectivities of the women of al-Hilal, particularly how they distinguish among the religious, the secular, and the political. These activist women's visions of Islamic piety, social change, and relationship to religion and political secular ideals are evident in their narratives and activism. They navigate seamlessly between religion and secularism; yet as disciplined citizens of a secularizing state, they distinguish in concrete terms their Islamic faith from government and law.

Islamic women's activism is part of the discourses of modernity and postcoloniality, and the activists' subjectivities are shaped and produced by changes in social institutions, such as the rise of capitalism, industrialization, global market economies, and the apparatuses that create and make these discourses hegemonic. Central to these processes is the growing bureaucratization and the expansion of the state into everyday life, as well as the increasingly complex divisions of secular modernity. This work assumes as a point of departure, however, that human beings are embodied, desiring, agential, and speaking subjects. I argue that the desires and subjectivities of the women who participate in Islamic activism in Egypt today are continuously produced by the histories characterizing their social present, and through the Islamic activism that shapes and is shaped by these desires.

Many of these women who participate in the Islamic movement in Cairo moved seamlessly between concomitant religious and secular practices. In their discourses they often mirrored the modernist ideal of defining clear boundaries between the realm of the religious and that of the political. Although they view Islam first as a religion and second as a social system, they describe religion as private and politics as public, which contradicts contemporary Islamic discourses, in which Islamists define Islam as *din wa dawla* (religion and state), or both a religion and a state. While the nation-state expands its control over the country's administrative, social, and cultural institutions, Islamic women activists often assume an ambiguous position from these imperatives of modernity. That is, they often distinguish themselves as apolitical and concerned only with issues of Islamic *mo'amalat.*[6]

Egypt's modernizing schemes are aimed at improving such areas as education, the position of women, and family planning. Furthermore, many activist women at al-Hilal have naturalized the state's views on education, child rearing, family relations, divorce, and marriage, despite their claims to follow religion in all that they do. The British colonial authority in Egypt ordered and disciplined the bodies and minds of the Egyptian people through modern education, policing, censuses, registration of births and deaths, and new ideas on health and hygiene centering on medical inspections of bodies and campaigns to eradicate diseases. Timothy Mitchell (1988) maintains that the emancipation of women, the education of the people, and the rights and legality of citizenship were accepted by the emerging Egyptian educated classes through Arabic-language periodicals, newspapers, and novels. Thus colonial history and nationalist state projects of modernization shaped, modified, and produced subjectivities and desires that led to an understanding of Islam and Islamic activism that cannot be separated from these processes. My work invites these considerations of the scholarship of women in Islamic movements, who are normalized in the literature as either liberatory or not, empowered or disempowered, and progressive or regressive, depending on how religious or secular they are. This research points to the importance of problematizing the notions of religious versus secular subjectivities not as contradictory but as mutually imbricated and multilayered. The construction of what is Islamic and what is secular is contingent on the exclusion and reification of boundaries based on earlier European colonialist projects and liberal modern projects of development adopted by the nation-state. According to Nilfur Göel's work on Islamic practices in Turkey, self-presentation is mediated by histories and discourses contingent on time and space. She points out the importance of understanding Islamic practices for a nuanced view of the public sphere, not just the space itself, but also the field that creates subjects through power. In this, Göel underscores the "unspoken, implicit borders and the stigmatizing, exclusionary power structure of the secular public sphere" (Göel 2002, 178).

— 6 —

Development and
Social Change

Mehmeit

The sounds of animated conversation filtered in from the outside as one after another a group of women walked into al-Hilal's spacious, freshly painted and carpeted meeting room. It was bright, with sunlight coming in through two big windows that faced the doorway. A long meeting table with a lace imitation plastic tablecloth surrounded by white plastic chairs dominated the room. On the walls, embroidered Islamic verses hung in gilded wooden frames, and in the corner, a three-panel screen propped against the wall caught my attention. The panels were decorated with ribbons of various colors, and someone had arranged a bouquet of artificial flowers in the center of each panel. The screen looked older than the rest of the furniture and appeared to have seen much use over time. Later I observed that it was used as a partition when more than one meeting was being held in the room. While I stood admiring the handiwork, a number of women came in and sat down around the long meeting table.

As they settled in, greeting one another, some of them put down their cell phones on the table in front of them. Then everyone's attention turned to Hagga Rabi'a. In her mid-fifties, she had been working at al-Hilal for more than four years. Hagga Rabi'a started the meeting by asking, "How will we get there?" There was no written agenda or summary of what was to be covered, as everyone already knew the purpose of the meeting: organizing a visit to a group of elderly people at a home in the countryside.

Hagga Nadia, who sat at the other end of the table, replied that they would rent a bus to take them there. "A bus?" asked Hagga Rabi'a. "I haven't rented a bus." As she talked, she looked through a notebook and began calling someone on her cell phone. She spoke in muted tones into her phone while the others continued the conversation.

In a few minutes, Hagga Rabi'a had rented a bus and began planning the excursion. She did not go around the table, nor did anyone raise their hands or take turns. Soon they had finished their plans. Laila, who also was attending the meeting, sat at a desk working on sending three thousand blankets to Aswan, an upper Egyptian city two hundred miles south of Cairo. During a cell phone conversation, she called out some suggestions to the women at the table. I had never been to a meeting like this, I thought to myself. Within fifteen minutes, the meeting was over. Some of the activists lingered behind to continue conversations; others finished their prayers in the corner; and a few talked to Laila at her desk. I was puzzled, knowing that it had taken so little time to organize what would have taken us three meetings to accomplish where I worked. I realized that these women's social networks enabled them to plan these events in the shortest amount of time possible. Still, the casual atmosphere and the lack of apparent structure—even though a structure was obviously in place—left me wondering.

This meeting brought to my attention women's Islamic activism that goes beyond the *gam'iyah* to the spaces and people in need of assistance. In the following, I discuss al-Hilal's work in a village that I call Mehmeit. There I saw how modern liberal principles of development and the imbricated values of the secular modern are applied on a grassroots level. I accompanied a group of women who worked at Mehmeit to observe how they interacted with the village women, the nature of their projects, and their vision of development. The work of two women, Amal and Samira, at Mehmeit was proudly described by the rest of the activists at al-Hilal as selfless *kheir* (good) for God's blessing. The older activist women, most of whom had visited Mehmeit, often discussed admiringly the efforts of these two to eradicate poverty in Egypt's rural areas.

Mehmeit, a Village of Many Possibilities

Twenty miles down the Nile from Cairo lies the village of Mehmeit. The rural areas surrounding Cairo are sites of human hardship, where poverty reigns and people struggle to survive without always having access to such basic necessities as food, clothing, and decent housing. Except for its interest to al-Hilal activists, it is like many such villages along the river. Mud-brick houses line the dirt roads of the village that seems to be sparsely populated, as most of its inhabitants are out in the field or at the local market.

Amal and Samira led al-Hilal's work on sustainable development in the village. Abdel Hamid al-Ghazali, a prominent Islamic scholar of economics, a member of the Muslim Brotherhood, and a professor of economics at Cairo University, described the principles of Islamic social development as follows:

> The Islamic system condemns poverty and promotes the practical struggle against it, to the extent that the Messenger of Allah, peace be upon him, prayed to Allah to guard him against poverty, equating it with unbelief. Islam attacked poverty with the aim of eradicating it. Work is considered to be an act of worship and social solidarity a fundamental principle of Islam. Together they act to achieve self-sufficiency. Based upon the objectives of *Shari'a*, all permissible actions, ritual or temporal, of the legally responsible Muslim constitute acts of worship. The act of worship, for which mankind has been created, is not expressed in Islam through laicitism [from *laïcité*, secularism], hermeticism and isolation, but through acting in accordance with the will of Allah to develop life on earth. Economic development is, therefore, a religious duty which must be carried out until the Day of Judgment. (Al-Ghazali 1994, 29)

Al-Ghazali emphasizes the Islamic concern with eradicating poverty and equating work with worship thus forging strong links between the divine, the individual, and the community. He makes a strong case, shared by the women of al-Hilal, for the religious obligation of economic development. Al-Ghazali is careful to distinguish between Islamic worship and French secularism, traditions of monasticism, and those he associates with isolation from social responsibilities.

As a prominent member of the Muslim Brotherhood, al-Ghazali emphasizes community development, which the Brotherhood also demonstrates in its commitment to an extensive network of development projects around the country. This commitment has both bolstered the Brotherhood's popularity with the masses and simultaneously weakened its position with the state, which regards the Brotherhood with hostility and suspicion.

Both al-Ghazali and the women of al-Hilal describe their social activism in religious terms that refer to divine ordinance, heavenly reward, and the principles and ethics of Islamic teaching. The ethnographic material that I gathered from my fieldwork at Mehmeit and the *gam'iyah* of al-Hilal attests to the subtle imbrication in their activism, of embedded liberal secular values and principles of modernization propagated by Egypt's colonialist and nationalist regimes. As subjects of a modernizing state whose institutions focus on the inculcation of modern liberal values in its population, the women of al-Hilal reflect a complex matrix of Islamic notions of development as worship and liberal modern schemes of development that have become appropriated and normalized as part of their Islamic discourse. As previously noted, although some of these modern liberal ideals are not in themselves alien to Islamic principles, their similarities and differences are not the basis of my argument here.

Instead, I am trying to show how activist women weave these various threads, inculcated by decades of modernizing projects and mutually embedded historically, into what to them is a coherent body of principles undergirding an activism that they define as Islamic. It is equally important not to gloss over the discontinuities and inconsistencies in all these processes. Whether on an individual or a social level, socializing processes and subject production are not an assembly-line production. As Gilles Deleuze and Félix Guattari (2004) remind us, the modern subject, desire, and individuality are "simply" heterogeneous. Claims that certain traits are related to a particular ideology or a specific cultural origin are misleading, as discursive traditions like Islam and liberal modern principles are themselves rhizomatic and cannot be isolated from their mutually embedded history. If we try to isolate them, we will risk essentializing each discourse. In contrast, we cannot lose sight of the genealogical historical processes that preceded the emergence of these traditions, since history, too, does not correspond to linear or stable trajectories or absolute anachronisms.

The activist women of al-Hilal were in their third year of social work. In the descriptions of their work, the embedded principles evident in their activism, and in their attitudes toward the village women can be described as what Foucault (1977) termed the modern techniques of discipline that imposed liberal values in Europe. These were designed primarily to "increase production, to develop the economy, spread education, raise the level of public morality; to increase and multiply" (Foucault 1977, 208). Egypt also was at the receiving end of these disciplinary reforms, as I showed in chapter 3, as part of both its colonial and its nation-state building history. Institutions such as schools, hospitals, factories, and the military comprised the machinery of modernity, aimed at inculcating order, awareness of time, scheduling, productivity, and self-fashioning as means of upward social mobility and achievement. The domestic sphere was a space for instilling these disciplinary values in women and young girls as the mothers of the nation and of future generations. The home was no longer closed to state intervention, and its institutions and discursive techniques were restructured to emphasize the values of domestic efficiency, as exemplified in modes of disciplining children, hygienic practices, and the production of the body as disciplined and docile. More important, the domestic was structured as the space where religion was to be produced as a private phenomenon, separate from the secular political public sphere. The production of subjectivity in Egyptian homes reinforced the liberal secular norm of separating the domestic and the political in principle, although in practice these demarcations were all too porous.

At Mehmeit, Amal and Samira demonstrated how these liberal secular norms were embedded in what they described as the religious duty they performed for their God. In their vision to develop this poor rural community, their goals and organizational plan often displayed the disciplinary techniques promoted by the state's modernizing projects. These techniques were evident in the Mehmeit project through the regulation of behavior by systematic supervision and the restructuring of daily activities, timed sessions, and scheduling, as well as an attendance record–taking system designed to evaluate the progress and degree of the village women's commitment to development.

A contractual relationship was the basis of the exchange between the Islamic women activists and the village women. In return for their commitment to attending religious lessons, literacy classes, practicing hygiene, and working on several types of production, the village women were rewarded with gifts and monthly wages and were given an opportunity to receive loans toward their financial independence. Through this contract, the al-Hilal women placed value on the Mehmeit women's economic productivity and often encouraged them to maintain their commitment to the project even when this was against their husband's desire. Although the contractual relationship exists in both Islamic society and liberal secular societies, its particular deployment in the Mehmeit project, with its emphasis on exchange, reward, and individual autonomy, should not be conflated with the kind of "mediated subjectivity" characteristic of some modern discourses on subjectivity in Islamic thought. According to Farzin Vahdat (2003, 6), the understanding of mediated subjectivity in Islamic thought is as a dual, schizophrenic relationship with the divine.[1]

An emphasis on education, hygienic practices, punctuality, and consistent attendance all were values the activist women sought to foster among the villagers. Although arguably Islamic objectives, these practices are historically part of the secularizing political schemes of nation-state building, merged seamlessly with Qur'anic recitals, religious lessons, and the various Islamic anecdotes designed to discipline and motivate the village women.

Amal and Samira keep detailed records of the eighty-nine households they oversee. Spreadsheets record each household member's name, age, and marital status, attendance at religious and literacy classes, diligence in following the prescribed hygiene practices, and even the cleanliness of each home. The records also show the number of house inspections to determine how each village woman maintains cleanliness and hygienic practices. The women of al-Hilal abolished the rural custom of keeping farm animals and humans under one roof, by providing funding to each family to build animal sheds separate from living areas. Samira keeps this information in a ledger she carries around with her in a big tote bag. The importance to al-Hilal of keeping records is determining the Mehmeit women's commitment to development and thus their eligibility for a loan to start a small business of their own.

Hence, attendance in weekly religious lessons and twice-a-week literacy classes is also taken. Another record measures the village women's productivity according to the number of products they each complete every week, which determines how much each woman is paid at the end of the month:

> We have to scrutinize each *hala* [case] to determine whether the women who has applied for the loan, first, has no source of income and, second, is a responsible person who will actually use the loan for herself and her family's sustainable living. Women who are not responsible and are not punctual and present in the various classes we offer are often refused loans.

Subjectivity, Discipline, and Social Change

The Mehmeit development program is clearly aimed at producing a particular subjectivity of the women of the village. Emerging from Amal's and Salmira's records are the outlines of a female Muslim ideal representing the principles of Islamic tradition, which focus on piety and dedication to Islamic teaching and learning, which merge with the liberal secular emphasis on discipline, autonomy, independence, and individual productivity. To illustrate how these embedded ideals drive the Mehmeit program and the process of subject formation that inculcate these values in the village women, let us consider how the project began, which is of particular interest. Amal described their first meetings with the women from Mehmeit, in which she and Samira were shocked to discover how "apathetic" the women were:

> After Samira and I settled on the choice of Mehmeit for the development project, we invited the women to come to a meeting in the town center so we could find out what their needs were. We also were looking to see what kinds of skills they already had so we could build on them to improve the living conditions in the village. Sherine, you have no idea the kind of poverty these women have to endure. When we first visited some of the homes, it was after bouts of heavy rain. Many of the palm reeds they use for roofing had rot-

ted, and worms were falling from the rotting ceilings into their food. The young children would pick out the worms, flick them away, and continue eating. It was appalling that they were living under these conditions.

We announced our first meeting, and when word spread across the village, we had a hall full of women. After explaining who we were and our project to help their village, we asked them whether they had any special skills or talents that we could help them develop, like sewing or clay making or anything like that. Our intention was to help them develop these skills to produce items we could sell for them in order to bring them some revenue.

The women just starred at us blankly. [Amal slumped in her seat, putting on a blank stare of her own to show me how the women acted.] They seemed so lazy and unwilling to do anything. Not a single one raised their hand or showed any interest. They truly did not understand that we were there to help them. But then we had an idea! We would use a reward system to motivate them. Can you imagine? A simple cotton *galabiyya*[2] made all the difference. . . . [Samira sounded sad and embittered in the face of such poverty.] Those who had special skills then started to get a bit animated. The reward worked, so we made it part of our project in order to get involved in all the other activities. They just could not see that becoming literate or learning about religion or any of that had any use in their lives. I do not blame them, as I would be like that, too, if I lived the life that they did.

When they returned to Cairo from that meeting, Amina and Salwa were very demoralized, feeling defeated even before they had started, but the support of other women activists gave them hope. The more experienced women at other organizations who carried out this sort of development in the villages gave them advice on ways of organizing that would ensure that the village women did not work just for the rewards and then leave but that they would establish a relationship with them that could then be sustained without the rewards. Brainstorming helped the women devise a new strategy based on a three-step plan, one that followed the system that Doctora Zeinab used at al-Hilal.

Part of the plan would be directed at the women's homes to raise their awareness of cleanliness. Weekly inspections would determine whether the women were maintaining hygienic practices. After being equipped with a clean water trough, underground container, and electricity, each house had to be swept, trash put out, and various other details, such as making sure that areas serving as toilets would be placed far from eating and sleeping quarters and that a pitcher of water and a bar of soap and a clean towel would always be available next to the toilet.

Animals would no longer be allowed in the house (Egyptian villagers traditionally allow their cows and buffaloes in their house while they often sleep outside or on the roof, because the animals are so important to their livelihood.) Trash was to be placed in large barrels outside the house, and al-Hilal activists arranged for the trash to be picked up. Sleeping quarters would be private. Girls' beds were separated from boys' beds because as Samira pointed out, "It is not Islamic to have the whole family sleeping in the same room. You have no idea the complications and problems these sleeping arrangements may cause."

The second phase of the plan was concerned with teaching the women sewing, basket making, or knitting. Each village woman who signed up for the training program had to attend a religious class once a week and a literacy class twice a week where hygiene and cleanliness issues were addressed. In addition, the villagers were to attend craft classes, from which the finished products were later sold at charity bazaars and the proceeds were put toward the small payments to the village women and also toward microfinancing qualified women.

Only later did Amal and Samira realize that making money was not a familiar experience to the women of Mehmeit, and they ended up giving the money to their husbands. When Amal discovered this, she spent many hours explaining to the women that this money is intended to provide for them and for their family's needs and not for their husbands to spend at the local coffee shop. I heard Amal raise her voice for the first time ever, one day, in the workshop in Mehmeit. "Your husband did not want you to leave your house? What do you mean? He just decides like that? To keep you at home? Well, tell him he will not see a penny from your work anymore! Who will pay for his *shisha*?"[3] The woman she was talking to was smiling shyly, knowing that she was now the center of attention. She argued feebly with Amal in what she knew was a losing battle, shrugging her shoulders and shaking her head from side to side at her husband. Her name was Nawal, and she lived in a two-bedroom mud-brick home very far from the center. Although her husband, Elewa, was ostensibly a farmer, he preferred to send Nawal to the field while he stayed home or visited with friends downtown. Samira explained to me that most of the men in Mehmeit did the same. Despite this injustice, Nawal did not complain:

> I still have to do the housework. I clean the house and cook and take care of the animals. The two days I work at the center are a nice time away from the backbreaking labor in the field. I see the other women; we chat and have a good time. But there were days when Elewa was sick and I just had to miss the classes.

The third aspect of al-Hilal's development project was providing the financial means for the village women to begin their own businesses, buy a plot of land, or eventually gain access to employment, all of which required start-up money. Samira and Amal examined the applicants' cases, making recommendations based on the women's financial need, how often they attended classes, how clean their homes were, and how well they worked. One day I watched an exchange with one of the applicants.

Khadra, an older village woman of about sixty, walked into the center at Mehmeit and, in a very loud voice, proceeded to chide Samira for not agreeing to finance her project for an underground reservoir of water, a project that Samira already had begun in the village. As the woman complained, Samira calmly responded by telling her that she could not have the loan because she already owned a third of a *feddan* (a *feddan* is a unit of land close to an acre) and that others who had nothing deserved the loan more. But the woman would not listen to her reasoning and, with a smile on her face, asked the same question again. Although Samira's face turned red, she was patient with the woman. After this exchange continued for a quarter of an hour, Samira finally gave the woman a harsh lesson in the proper Islamic way of acting honestly and fairly toward others. Her reply was swift and decisive and left no doubt in the woman's mind that she would never receive a loan. I was surprised to see the village woman still smiling when she left the center, saying that she would be back. Samira laughed and said, "Fine, but you still won't get the loan." Then turning to me, she said that this had been going on for months.

These glimpses into the interactions between the village women and Amal and Samira were of great interest to me. It was clear that that both women were dedicated and hardworking and did what they could to accomplish their goals. Amal's and Samira's role was that of an authoritarian, urban professional who knew how to improve the lives of the "simple" villagers. Although they must have realized that this role set them apart and that they had to give orders rather than rule by consensus, they always were sympathetic to the women of Mehmeit. Although they saw their role as the director of the project, they knew all the women by name and their circumstances quite intimately. In short, they did more for these women than any social worker employed by the government would do. Nevertheless, it was interesting to see the power dynamics in the village. My presence as a volunteer with the women of al-Hilal gave me a position of authority as well. Try as I might, it was almost impossible to escape this role, and once again I noted how the balance of power shifted in a new direction.

The first of my many visits to Mehmeit was on an early Tuesday morning. Amal and Samira were going to take me with them to the village. I was at our meeting point on time when Amal called me on my cell phone. She spoke a rich, articulate colloquial Arabic. Indeed, many of the women I met—Laila, Malak, and others—used an expressive Arabic, with a vocabulary that many colloquial speakers (myself included) do not muster. In any case, Amal gave the impression of a boundless energy that I immediately discovered at our first meeting. She announced that she would be in a car on the opposite side of the road. When I checked my watch, she was exactly on time. She told me to look for a white Peugeot station wagon, which in Cairo is a common means of transport between villages or from town to village.

The car was piled high with what appeared to be clothes, fabrics, and colorful baskets. I crossed the road to meet the four women, who were tightly packed inside the car with supplies on their laps and under their feet. Their driver, whom they called Khalil, obviously had been working with them for a while, for he called them by name and was familiar with the complicated way to Mehmeit by means of unmapped village roads.

Introductions followed as the car sped along the road to the village of Mehmeit in Middle Egypt. Amal sat next to me, Samira near the window, Nadia in the back, and Hagga Samiha in the front. Hagga Samiha was being sponsored to teach sewing to the village women. Amina and Salwa were in their late thirties to early forties. We talked excitedly together about our work and what they were trying to do at Mehmeit. For an hour and a half, which seemed like mere minutes when we arrived, I heard how Amal and Samira had started their project at Mehmeit. They chose the village because it was the most destitute one they could find this close to Cairo. When the car finally stopped at our destination, I could see why.

My first impression of Mehmeit was as another impoverished village, similar to many in the neglected countryside of Egypt whose survival to this day seems almost miraculous. Millions of people are forced to survive on a pittance with unstable employment and a lack of basic necessities such as food, clean running water, and electricity. The children of families in rural Egypt seldom went to school, as they are needed for work in order for the family to survive, with many earning less than a pound a day (twenty cents).

On Tuesdays in Mehmeit, the weekly market was held. People milled about the stalls talking and walking away with little. I looked at the products: soap, plastic combs, biscuits, and a limited variety of vegetables, mainly onions and potatoes. The marketplace was situated at an intersection, whose dirt roads the shopkeepers kept sprinkling with water to keep the dust off the merchandise. Along one side of the market ran a narrow canal with thick muddy water that flowed through the village, providing the only source of water for washing clothes and animals. As we hurtled along in our old wagon, debris and waste floated down the canal.

At last at our destination, I looked around and watched as a group of women and girls greeted Amal, Samira, Nadia, and Hagga Samiha. It was an exciting scene, with everyone chattering at once. Several rolls of colored fabric, towels, and linens were unloaded from the car, and big bags of clothes, colorful *galabiyyas*, and baskets were carried up the stairs of a half-finished two-story building by the waiting crowd. This building housed the development project at Mehmeit that Amal and Samira had started years ago, teaching the local women a skill that would help generate funds and support village households. The flight of stairs ended at a small apartment packed with quite a large group of twenty women from the village.

In one corner, a few women sat cross-legged on the floor making multicolored baskets that I had seen on display on the shelves at al-Hilal. In another well-lit corner around a long dining table, a group of younger-looking women worked with Nadia, making table mats that were ordered a month ago by a shop owner in the city. And on the sofas lined up against the walls, in the traditional village fashion, women sat face to face decorating towels and knitting a lace-like trimming, which they called *kroshé* (crochet). This scene immediately became animated as we walked through the door, with each of the city women taking a few minutes to greet and be greeted by the village women.

Amal, obviously now the leader of the group, called all the women to begin the day by reading verses from the Qur'an. Immediately, clearly and in unison, the thirty-plus women started reciting the *fatha*[4] and the small *suras* (verses) of the Qur'an. I was reminded of my school days when our Arabic teacher would have us recite similar verses during religion class. We all would stumble and mumble here and there over the difficult parts, but these village women, many of whom were still learning to read and write, did not miss a beat. Their intonations were in step, the words rolling off their tongues with the clarity of a bell. I both marveled and felt embarrassed to be witnessing this, since I was not a part of it, and I also felt slightly awkward, for I knew they were also watching me curiously to see if I knew the verses. My lips began to move along with theirs, but try as I might, I could not meet their perfect rhythm and felt self-conscious until, to my relief, the recital finally ended.

Then Amal spoke, saying that she was proud that many of them were following the rules of cleanliness and hygiene that she and Samira had been trying to teach them. She took out her ledger. I stared in amazement at the lists of women, with their children's names, ages, and descriptions of their homes; weekly attendance at religious classes and literacy lessons; and hygiene checks of eighty-nine houses. Amal announced that they had brought *galabiyyas* for those who had faithfully attended their classes and kept their homes clean and in order. One woman who did not receive a *galabiyya* seemed particularly disappointed and shyly approached Amal, explaining that she had missed two religion classes because she had to take care of her mother-in-law who was sick and had no one to tend her but herself. Amal listened to her and reached into the bag and handed her a *galabiyya*, cautioning the woman this would be her last time to miss class. Another younger women, emboldened by what had transpired, went up to Amal and also asked for a *galabiyya*. Amal asked her name and consulted her ledger. But shaking her head, Amal told her she would not receive a *galabiyya* today, since she had missed several classes and had to understand that this is a two-way street for her to show how responsible she could be so that she could continue working at the center. The young woman made a feeble attempt at a commonly used reason for not attending class—that her husband kept her at home. Amal was firm.

> If your husband does not want you here, then you will not make the money you contribute to your family every month, and you will not learn to read and write or any of the skills we teach you here. It is as simple as that. For now, go to your classes, and next time you will get your gift.

Although Amal was quite understanding of the first woman's reason for missing class, she clearly rejected the second woman's excuse that her husband had kept her at home. Taking care of an elderly in-law was to Amal an obligation that she approved of, even encouraged. But a husband who refused to let his wife go to religion class was not a valid reason to her. In fact, she was short with the younger women who used this excuse, as if to set an example for the others. Her response was based on the contract between the village women and al-Hilal. Attendance at religious lessons was an indication of commitment. Even though religious aims were not part of the contract, money was exchanged in return for productivity, despite the project's

Islamic ethic. This emphasis on individual contractual relations attests to one of the main ways in which the liberal secular ethic of individuality, freedom, and independence follows the contractual principal that requires individuals to exchange their labor for wages. Undoubtedly, this principle was not easy for the women in the village of Mehmeit to accept.

The Mehmeit project afforded a glimpse into the practical side of Islamic women's activism. I noticed how their activism affected the larger community of women in remote rural areas of Egypt. Amal spoke directly to the women, slightly raising her voice in order to be heard, and they listened closely to her. Often the younger women had a look of admiration on their faces as she pointed out that Islam emphasized the values of education, hygiene, and productivity. Their faces lit up when she called them by their name or asked them a question. To them, Amal was a model of Islamic womanhood that they all wished to emulate. Urban, educated, and obviously more financially prosperous than they were, she embodied qualities to which the village women aspired. They believed that the program would make them just like her.

When the session was over and the women started working on their arts and crafts for the next bazaar, it was time to do the rounds. I followed Amal outside as we walked along the dirt roads of Mehmeit, going from door to door.

We visited about ten homes that day. Amal went into each, inspecting bathrooms, bedrooms, and the rest of the house as each housewife proudly displayed her housekeeping skills. All the houses were built out of mud brick, and some were lime-washed in shades of white, green, and blue. None of the houses we visited had floors. Instead, the ground was covered with compacted mud that was often sprinkled with water to keep the dust down. Most of the homes contained an entrance hallway that also served as an animal pen, followed by the sitting area, which doubled as a dining space where a *tablia* (a round, short-legged table) would be brought out and around which the family would gather, sitting on the straw floor mat to share their meal. Most of the sleeping quarters were next to the entrance, and in the better-off households, built-in beds were lined against the walls and covered with clean sheets. In the poorer houses, mats were rolled out on the floor. The houses' mud-brick architecture was designed to keep them cool: the walls were whitewashed, the windows were placed high to keep out the dust and heat and also to keep the house cool and dark. The atrium around which the house was built and onto which the rooms opened, varied in size. This was where the women worked, baking, washing (if they had running water, which was rare), and cooking.

The same routine was repeated in each home we visited. One of the women would rush to the entrance (many of the homes did not have doors) and welcome us. Amal, looking as efficient as a health inspector, would walk in, ledger and pen in hand. She profusely complimented the women when she found them to be hardworking and clean, but she could just as easily resort to stern disapproval with those who did not follow her hygiene expectations. One of the women did not have soap next to the toilet. Amal gently rebuked her and insisted that she go out that instant and get soap. As we waited for the woman to return from the store, Amal turned to me and said, "If I don't do this, they won't care and they will take me for granted. They want to get out of their commitments. If it were up to them, they'd just take the rewards and run. It's human nature."

Amal paid special compliments to Om Ahmed (*om* means the mother of Ahmed; women in the Egyptian countryside are often addressed by the name of their oldest son). Nonetheless, most of the village women I met at the center and in our walks through the village were called by their first names. Without taking census of the households, Amal and Samira would have a hard time keeping track of women named Om Ahmed or Om Mohamed, since Ahmed and Mohamed are very common names.

Om Ahmed

Om Ahmed's mud-brick home was indeed the tidiest and cleanest one I saw in Mehmeit. All the floors were swept clean, and the dust was momentarily under control. The beds were made, the sheets looking crisp and fresh and the blankets folded neatly at the foot of the narrow mattresses. The bathroom in the back had a plastic cup and a bar of soap next to the porcelain in-ground squatting toilet, and a clean towel hung from a hook in the wall. I noticed that the bathroom had a sink and a faucet, so I asked Om Ahmed about that, since I had not seen them in any of the other houses. Om Ahmed, a very short woman of about forty, with weather-beaten skin that made her look older, crossed her thin arms across her stomach in a customary gesture and said to me, "*Mahu da min kheir al-Doctora*" (This is all from the goodness of the doctor [meaning Amal]).[5] But Amal replied with a half smile, "*Ya Om Ahmed da min kheir Rabina!*" (Om Ahmed, this is from God's bounty!). Om Ahmed started to object but thought better of it and continued to discuss the well that al-Hilal had helped her build behind her house. She explained to me that al-Hilal had lent her about two hundred Egyptian pounds (US$40) to buy two goats. She fed the goats, sold the goat milk, and eventually sold their kids. When she had enough money, she bought more goats, and so on. Amina encouraged Om Ahmed and helped her borrow money for the well so she and her family could have clean water in their home. Om Ahmed was now making enough money from her goat business to pay off the loan and buy a cow, which was a very big deal to her. "I never thought I could ever afford a cow; this is a dream come true!" I could not help thinking as I watching Om Ahmed's beaming face telling me about the cow how fascinating it was how desire is produced. Om Ahmed's desire for a cow took her through a long disciplinary process that put her on the road towards her dream but also led to new desires in her that started her down other paths. Through this process, she learned how to write her name and recite verses from the Qur'an. She diligently followed al-Hilal's instructions, keeping her house clean and tidy and her bathroom in order. Her goats were an extra responsibility, but they brought rewards. I cannot imagine what it was like for Om Ahmed to work so hard for four years to attain her dream. Now with the beautiful brown cow in her yard, Om Ahmed's had a well enabling her to do her laundry at home and not have to walk down to the muddy river. With this sense of achievement, a belief reinforced by the fruits of her labor, anything, in her world, was possible. What would she dream of tonight? I asked her, "What is your biggest wish, *ya Om Ahmed?*" She replied, "I want electricity, *ya doctora*, so my children can study at night and I can watch television. The gas lamp is weakening their eyesight."

Halima

Amal and Samira ensured that the Mehmeit program ran smoothly in their absence by hiring a man from the village who acted as the program's manager and reported back to them by telephone. Ahmed graduated from high school in 1976 and wanted to go to college to become a schoolteacher and maybe even a headmaster, but he had seven younger brothers and sisters that he had to take care of. His father was too old to tend to their small plot of land, so Ahmed went to the city, Cairo, or Masr,[6] and soon found a job as a clerk in an accounting office to help make ends meet. He sent money home every month and commuted on weekends and vacations. Soon after getting married he and his wife started to have children, who remained in the village with their mother. When Ahmed's father died, Ahmed moved back to Mehmeit and took care of the small plot of land. But even though he was well respected by the villagers and was in many ways at the head of his small community, he always missed the city and his old job. When Amal and Samira began organizing the Mehmeit center of al-Hilal, he offered his services, and the two found him to be a well-organized and dependable ally.

Ahmed's eldest daughter, Halima, who was about twenty years old, took over most of the work in the village when her father went on official errands in the city. Like her father, Halima knew everyone by name without the help of a ledger because she had grown up in Mehmeit and knew all the village families well. One of her many tasks was to notify Amal and Samira when a family fell on hard times and needed help. Another of Halima's duties was to supervise the religious lessons, take attendance, and report back. In return for a monthly wage that was considered by village standards a good sum of money, Halima, her father, and two other women from the village conducted the home inspections during the week. I talked with Halima about her work with al-Hilal as we walked toward the weaving center on a warm winter day. Halima was dressed in a bright apple green hybrid between a dress and a *galabiyya*. Although more tailored, it still was long and flowing like a *galabiyya*. Like many of the village women, her hair was in two long braids. She had a pretty round face and was very animated. Halima told me that she made a good monthly salary compared with that of other people in Mehmeit, enabling her to save for the day she would be married.

> It makes me happy doing what I do, because for the first time in my life I am given an important job like this. My father insisted that I finish my education. I have my *shihada*,[7] and I can write and read fluently. I can keep the records for Doctora Amal and Doctora Samira. It is enjoyable work because I spend my day visiting and calling on people. It is not a boring job, and I do not have to work at home anymore, as the other girls my age do. My mother and my younger sisters do that, and I help them sometimes, of course.
>
> People respect me because I work with the center. What is best for me is when I go to Masr. It is just a thrill. I sometimes have to take a sick person myself to see a doctor. I make all the contacts on my own. I call the doctor's office before I go and make all the arrangements. It is important work.

Halima's work and her pleasure and confidence in it were, according to her, for only one purpose:

> I want to be married one day and move to Cairo. I do not want to marry someone who is less than me, like someone who is not educated or not from the same kind of family background. I hope to find *shirik hayaty*[8] and get married and have our own apartment.

Occasionally as we walked through the village alleys, we met old women who sat on the floor, huddled in doorways. Many of them seemed thin and shriveled. Their black *galabiyyas*, dusty and tattered, covered their jutting bones. Amal explained to me that the village's extreme poverty forced many to turn their backs on their family obligations, like honoring the elderly. Most of the elderly in the village were widowed women who had no source of income to support themselves. In many cases, the old women were abandoned and left to live the last years of their lives in the basement of houses or under the stairwell of mud-brick homes. Amal described the miserable state in which she found some of the women. They were sitting in excrement, with bedsores all over their bodies, half starved, and sick.

Amal and Samira decided to set aside money to support these women. Using their contacts from the medical profession, they formed a network of physicians to provide medical care for them. Consequently, yet another list in their ledger contains the names, ages, address, and medical and social condition, including medications, of all the elderly women in Mehmeit. Halima checks on them every day to make sure they have been fed and bathed, and if they need medical help, she contacts either Amal or Samira, who makes an appointment for them with one of the network's doctors. So far, Amal told me, they have taken care of eighteen neglected women. She mentioned how difficult it sometimes was to talk to the family members, who barely had a roof over their head, about taking care of a sick old woman when they could not even feed their children. In those cases in which the neglect was avoidable, Amal used shame to make the families pay attention. Although she gave each of these families money to support the old women, sometimes it was only shame that moved them to act.

Productive Entrepreneurs in Mehmeit

Still, I was to discover even more about al-Hilal's development program at Mehmeit. Samira had set up and ran a carpet-weaving workshop in a one-story building a few meters away from the center. She was particularly proud of the organization of the production in the workshop as she showed me around the five rooms where the weaving looms were housed. The place was spotless compared with the rest of the village, which was literally covered in dirt and trash. Here at the weaving center, I saw order and organization. About twelve young women were seated on benches, their carpets in front of them. They were working from designs on papers attached to the wall, their fingers moving quickly on their looms as they worked in unison.

The carpet-weaving project was testimony to the resourcefulness and organizational capabilities of the women of al-Hilal and the superb skills of the women of Mehmeit. Despite its similarity to the various weaving workshops set up for tourists in Saqqara, Kerdasa and Akhmim, where rural subjects were disciplined into production for the business owner's gain, in Mehmeit, the revenue went back to the village and its families. I wondered whether Amal and Samira contemplated giving the weavers control over their production.

Samira explained to me that Ali, a professional carpet maker from Cairo, agreed to come down to Mehmeit in return for a good salary and a place to stay. He set up the weaving project and trained the girls himself. In a matter of a few months, the carpet-weaving project began to yield a profit.

The girls who worked as weavers were making considerably more money than the others making baskets and sewing. They, too, were required to attend the literacy classes and the weekly religious lessons. Donya, a sixteen-year-old girl, told Samira that her father had forbidden her to come to work again. This worried Samira, who told the distraught young woman that she would talk to Hagga Samiha, who knew her father and she would talk to him on her behalf.

As we talked and inspected the carpets, we heard the call for midday prayer. The girls stopped and sat around Samira in a big circle. Samira wanted to give them a few minutes to talk about science. She brought out a few beautiful pictures of planets and stars that she had copied from the Internet and held them up. "See?" she asked. "The power of Allah is great. Not even the United States knows everything about outer space. The Americans have gone to the moon and sent rockets across the earth, but they still cannot measure the power of God." Samira went on to talk about the planets and the stars, giving the girls a lesson in astronomy. At the end of class, Samira asked them to recite some *suras* (verses) from the Qur'an and then distributed their lunch.

When they were finished eating, the girls went across the hall to perform their ablutions and came back quickly. As they got ready to begin praying, their eyes were riveted on Samira. Finally, the small group stood shoulder to shoulder, with Samira at the front leading them in prayer.

Addressing the girls before the prayer, she emphasized the power of the creator and the importance of following him in their hearts in their daily lives. In her short lesson to the girls, she repeatedly stressed the importance of their commitment to development, education, and to being productive members of their community. She stressed hygiene and cleanliness, and indeed, the girls kept the workshop immaculate.

In her exchange with the girls, Samira emphasized achievement and the value of productivity and financial independence, and self-reliance. Her rhetoric captured a sense of the liberal modern as it is incorporated in Islamic discourse on ideal womanhood, which she herself exemplified to the girls and women of Mehmeit.

As I write, the Mehmeit project is now in its fourth year. The activists run the various classes and projects with precision and dedication that reflect the principles of the *gam'iyah* in Cairo. The Mehmeit project is a poignant example of the impact of Islamic activism in tackling poverty on the scale that I saw in this village. The administration of the Mehmeit project demonstrates the mutual imbrication of the discourses of Islam and secular modernity. Several themes relating to this issue stood out for me.

One was the contractual nature of the relationship between the village women and the al-Hilal women. The relationship was based on individual will and freedom of exchange, which was further solidified by gain, reward, and financial support. Clearly, the contract contained an economic factor from the liberal secular principles of the market in which the ability to contract labor becomes an embodiment of freedom and autonomy (Robbins 1961, 104). This view claims that the freedom is the ability to enter into contracts and freely employ one's gains. The village women of Mehmeit were not familiar with these concepts. To them, the notion of gain was clear in principle but not in practice. Their first reaction to receiving wages was to give them to their husbands, to which activists of al-Hilal immediately objected. They made it clear that the women needed to decided on their own how to spend their earnings. They stressed the village women's independence and choice, to the point of chiding them if they gave in to their husband's pressure to stay home and neglect the center.

The initial challenge for al-Hilal women was the villagers' lack of desire to become involved in a project, which, to the activists, would improve the villagers' lives. It was not that the villagers were not desiring subjects; it was that they were not *modern* desiring subjects. They did not subscribe to the Islamic version of desire that al-Hilal inculcated in its participants. Accordingly, Amal and Samira had to produce a particular kind of desire to promote piety and Islamic principles. Om Ahmed epitomized the desiring subject in the Meh-meit project. Her motivated personhood was clearly engaged with the modern process of refashioning the self. This desire in self-fashioning made al-Hilal's project possible, as it emphasized the liberal secular values contained in the activists' Islamic vision of social development. The values and ethics that Amal and Samira sought to inculcate in the village women are reminiscent of the programs of modernization that colonialist administrations and national governments instilled in the educated classes. These programs value punctuality, self-disci-pline, hygienic practices, and effective household organization and, most important, individual material production and motivation, all of which were merged with both similar and contradictory Islamic prin-ciples and practices. At the same time, the power dynamics were clear between the women of al-Hilal, who acted as the "civilizing" force at Mehmeit, and the women of the village, who, they believed, were "lazy" and "unmotivated." These dynamics covered class, education, and even piety, qualities that gave al-Hilal women credibility and also positioned them as authoritative, powerful figures of social and cul-tural change, in their transactions with the villagers.

The written records that Amal carried in her tote bag enabled her to evaluate the village women's performance and hence determine the level of their commitment. These records acted in much the same way that the government census does, for their knowledge about the indi-viduals also gave them power and control.

The virtues of education and the importance of freedom of choice also paralleled the state's modernization projects. "Islam" was invoked in these practices every time a new concept was introduced and even when the village women attended a lesson on astron-omy. A religious rhetoric was always linked to the activities and discussions.

In their attempts to introduce the villagers of Mehmeit to sustain-able development, the women activists drew on their own desires and ideals. Disciplining the village's households was just one example of how the larger projects of modernization led by the state had found their way into their notion of development. Under an Islamic rubric, however, the al-Hilal women regarded these development schemes to improve the villagers' education, independence, and sustainability as a form of Islamic worship. As means of gaining closeness to their God, their principles of individuality and entrepreneurship intertwined with religious practice. The social development project in Mehmeit offered a range of possibilities for viewing the concomitance of religion and secularism. As it revealed the imbricated ideas of the individual, the community within the space in which the ideals of Islamic activism took shape, it captured al-Hilal women's vision for social change.

Reconsidering Women's
Desires in Islamic Movements

One evening in the spring of 2007, two women were sitting on a panel on either side of a faculty moderator facing an audience of students and scholars. The debate, sponsored by the political science department at the American University in Cairo, was entitled "Egyptian Women: Which Way Forward?" On the moderator's right side was the Islamic feminist Amany Abul Fadl, dressed in shades of white and wearing a long *khimar*[1] that extended down to her waist. On the moderator's left side was the liberal feminist activist Aida Seif al-Dawla, in a navy blazer and skirt.

The event started with each panelist describing her views of women's issues in Egypt. Both Abul Fadl and Seif al-Dawla were concerned with the challenging conditions under which women labor. They both agreed that the state did not support working women and that women were not represented politically in the country. The panelists took turns answering the audience's questions, each emphasizing her own position as Islamic or liberal with regard to the issue she was discussing. Often they were openly critical of each other's views. Abul Fadl, an avid supporter of the Muslim Brotherhood, accused nongovernment organizations (NGOs) (Seif al-Dawla works for the el-Nadim Centre for the Rehabilitation of Victims of Violence) of being mouthpieces of the West and of fostering Western views alien to Egyptian society. Seif al-Dawla was just as critical of the Muslim Brotherhood, maintaining that its exclusionary practices were just as discriminating as the state's and were not conducive to democracy. She also addressed Abul Fadl's criticism of NGOs by stating that never in her career had foreign funding forced her to pursue issues in which she was not interested, nor had she ever felt coerced by Western agendas. Seif al-Dawla is known to be an outspoken human rights activist who has occasionally staged hunger strikes to oppose government policies. Amany Abul Fadl has a similarly turbulent history with the state. Her apartment, she recounted, had often been ransacked by government secret police because of her affiliations with the Brotherhood, which is a banned Islamist group.

A few minutes into the discussion, a member of the audience asked about female genital mutilation (FGM).[2] FGM is a central issue in the debate on women's rights in Egypt and has caused public disagreement since CNN's 1994 graphic broadcast of the circumcision of a ten-year-old girl. Even though the grand sheikh of Al-Azhar University, Mohammed Sayyid Tantawi, has declared FGM to be un-Islamic, Sheikh Youssef al-Qaradawi, a leading Muslim Brotherhood scholar, has remained neutral toward the practice. However, in 1996, a national ban on FGM was enforced by the minister of health, Ismail Sallam. This does not mean, however, that FGM is no longer practiced in Egypt, and Abul Fadl described her frustration when she was unable to convince the janitor of her building not to send his three daughters back to the village to be circumcised. She exclaimed wryly, "The janitor now regards me as not a real Muslim, even though I assured him that Islam never required girls to be circumcised. But how can I single-handedly change his perceptions when he strongly believes that it has?"

Abul Fadl continued, explaining that it was difficult to dislodge age-old misconceptions and replace them with correct Islamic practices. Several hands shot up in the audience clamoring for a chance to ask Seif al-Dawla whether the NGOs she worked with had had any success in eradicating FGM. Seif al-Dawla's reply presented another dilemma. She was critical of the state's position, which, rather than dealing with engrained gender inequality, preferred to treat only symptomatic phenomena such as FGM. She explained that banning FGM has had even worse implications for girls whose parents, bent on ensuring their daughters' marital future, hire practitioners of FGM who continue to perform this inhumane task under dangerous and unsanitary conditions. This in turn has increased the incidence of infection and even death for these young women.

"I call for education. Education is the answer. You cannot expect people who are illiterate and uneducated to make sound decisions.

The government, which insists on keeping our population ignorant so they can do what they please, must understand that this is not acceptable," emphasized Abul Fadl, who herself holds a doctorate degree. She ended her call for reform with a cautionary note to Seif al-Dawla:

> I want to say one last thing to Dr. Seif al-Dawla: not everything is the result of gender inequality. Gender inequality is just a symptom of larger inequalities in society—inequalities that are ignored by the government. We have to open our eyes to the bigger issues in this country and not just remain transfixed on issues of gender and the veil.

The time was up, and Seif al-Dawla did not have time to respond. In fact, as I left the room with the rest of the crowd, I doubted whether she would have disagreed with Abul Fadl.

In public discourse, liberal and Islamic feminist activisms are reified as two distinct monoliths, a binary reinforced in the self-presentation and discursive techniques of the activists themselves. Presented as two opposing contenders, the panelists from each side of these perceived divides of Islamism and liberal secularism are seated on opposite ends of tables in public debates where Egypt's future is queried and probed. Despite the differences characterizing the speakers and emphasized in the event's presentation, unifying themes also were evident in the discourses we had just heard. Amany Abu Fadl has a feminist outlook and emphasized the importance of women having a political role in the country. Political participation is often seen as a luxury that not too many women in Egypt can afford (Chinoy 2006). She often blames the state, as does Aida Seif al-Dawla, for its violence against individuals. Educating the public is a priority to both women in their fight for democracy and human rights. More often than not, however, the struggle of each of these women is posited as a different feminist agenda. The Islamic scholar and activist Omaima Abou Bakr questioned the futility of these polarizing discourses:

> A recurrent and accentuated polarity seems to emerge between Islamic and secular feminism as lobbying for completely different demands. In my opinion, it would not serve the general cause of Arab/Muslim/Middle Eastern women to highlight the fact that two

such orientations are ideologically worlds apart and are to work separately in separate spheres. . . .

Islamic feminists engaged in reforming religious discourses and
practices concerning women are doing a greatly needed service to
the rest of activists and feminists, complementing their work in
development, civil rights, law reforms, reproductive health, circumcision, violence, discrimination, etc. (Abou Bakr 2001, 1)[3]

Analyses of the unitary ethical subjectivities of individuals in Islamic
movements today are not only unilinear and one dimensional but also
inaccurate. Although I argue that desire and subjectivity are always
heterogeneous and incomplete, I do not claim that the women of al-
Hilal represent all Islamic groups. In fact, I propose that the dynamics of desire are always contextual, contingent, and incomplete. I have
contended that desire is shaped by often contradictory constructions
in changing fields of power relations as Islamic movements propel
activists into new social arenas and discursive spaces.

Representations of Islamic activist women as caught between two
discourses of religion and liberal modernity are inadequate as well, for
understanding women's position in Islamic societies. The reason is not
only because religion and liberal modernity are not binaries but also
because women are not the powerless terrain on which these battles
are fought. The subjectivities and desires of women activists in Islamic
movements cannot be described as religious but, rather, as partly
shaped by the concomitance of Islamic practice and liberal secular
projects. My aim is to argue that religious practice is often shaped by
political and social processes that must be considered when discussing
religious traditions and subjectivities in the world today.

Women's Islamic Activism beyond the Secular-Religious Binary

Throughout this book I have tried to provide a more nuanced picture
of the experiences of the women who engage in Islamic activism, in
order to complicate the normative dichotomy between Islamic and
secular. Although they share some of the concerns voiced by Egyptian
feminists, Laila, Hagga Afaf, Samya, Amal, and the rest of the al-Hilal

women follow their own activist agenda. This agenda, as I showed in previous chapters, reflects an embedded concomitance of Islamic and secular liberal principles inculcated through the process of modernization by the colonialist and nationalist states. These women are challenging the meaning of what it is to be an Islamic activist in the contemporary world. They each have a story, told in coherent and consistent terms, which constructs them in the telling and builds the blocks of their lives.

As modern subjects of a so-called secularizing state, activist Islamic women experience and reproduce the projects of modernization, which in Egypt have been particularly interested in reordering female minds and bodies. The domestic space has always been crucial to reform projects, as Dipesh Chakrabarty (1992) pointed out. As women, they were taught to be the guardians of tradition and national identity. As housewives, they were expected to carry out their domestic chores in an organized modern fashion and practice scientific hygienic habits in their homes. Most important, they were to be the mothers of future generations and to raise their children as disciplined and obedient citizens. Islamic activist women such as Laila, Hagga Afaf, Samya, and Amal and the many others who work with them view their activism as work for God. Laila described her commitment to activism as "a marriage to someone that you love with all your heart."

The women of al-Hilal have educated themselves in Islamic teachings, spread the word of Islam as *da'iyat*,[4] perfected their religious practices, and organized Islamic development projects in poor, marginalized villages. Their desires and subjectivities embody the mutual embedded ideals of historically produced Islamic traditions and secular liberal projects of modernity. Each of their lives is a rich and multidimensional terrain on which their desires flow, merge, conflict, and follow no particular geography.

More significantly, theirs are not consistent stories that can be told merely as they tell them. I have argued that the women of al-Hilal can neither be understood in Islamic terms alone nor can be effectively captured through a normative liberal secular lens that assumes a demarcation between religion and secularism. In fact, as the data collected for this book show, the inseparability of these discourses, however much they may seem to be in conflict, are often a repository of resources for

Islamic activist women to draw on, to rethink norms and traditions, and to rebuild exciting opportunities and possibilities for change.

Escaping the confining rigors of the secular-religious binary enables an understanding of women's changing status in societies that are becoming increasingly Islamized. Women are not the passive terrain on which secularizing states and religious groups vie to gain control. Instead, women often engage with these multiple discourses in ways that may also translate into activism and not necessarily into passivity and oppression. Many feminist studies represent Islamic women as torn between traditional Islam and secularism as exemplified by modernizing regimes (al-Ali 2000; Badran 1991; Cole 1981; Fernea 2000; Hatem 1998; Ong 1990; Talhami 1996). In contrast, I argue that these constructs are mutually imbricated discourses of which women are a part and not a separate, passive entity. Aiwa Ong's argument that the secular state and Islamic groups are competing for the control of Malaysian society by defining women's bodies through the regularization of the domestic unit reinstates binaries that obscure the role of Malaysian women and constructs them as passive, disempowered victims. Mervat Hatem (1986) uses the same reasoning as Ong in her description of the situation in Egypt. According to Hatem, Islamists and the Egyptian state have traditionally regarded women as their negotiating tools for the control of personal status laws governing the family and women's domestic rights.

These approaches describe women's subjectivities as a terrain over which reified binary constructs of the state and Islamic groups are struggling to control. This theoretical scenario is true of Franz Fanon's (1967) masculinist racial battles over women's bodies, an analysis reducing women to the status of subalterns without adequate regard for the complexity of their experiences. Western colonialist thought, which normatively represents religion and secularism as opposing categories, invigorates these dichotomous assumptions and enables a systematic reduction of women into symbolic or discursive spaces over which political battles are fought. According to Marnia Lazreg (1994), in Algeria, French colonialists focused on women's bodies as the locus of occupation, seeing women's bodies as the symbolic space of occupation and the emasculation of Algerian masculinity. Consequently, Lazreg argues, the control of women's bodies later became the site for liberation movements. Both colonialists and liberators, she argued, reproduced women as a symbolic terrain over which their political struggle was played out. Representing women as caught between the binaries of Islamic practice and secularism echo these colonialist and nationalist constructs. Paradoxically, the literature describing women's plight under oppression appropriates these constructs and fails to account for the ways in which women actively shape the terrain of struggle.

In my analysis of women's desires in Islamic movements, I also contend that uncritically employing a category called *religion* to interpret Islamic practices and principles is inadequate, owing to the term's Western-centric nature and its close ties to the liberal secular project of modernity. Islamic tradition itself is discursive, not static, with regional diversity and cultural differences embedded in its practice. Liberal modernity, however, also assumes variation. Liberal secular projects in Egypt are not the same as those propagated by other postcolonialist and nation-states, nor are they identical to Western liberal modernity, which also, in itself, is not a monolith.

Furthermore, the failure to see the heterogeneity of desires among women engaging in Islamic movements and the rhizomatic ways in which they are shaped not only views the subjectivities of these women as one dimensional but also distorts the nature of women's Islamic activism. Desire is not a reified object that can be captured as a unified theme. Instead, desire allows an analysis of subjectivity that gets at the core of subject production and also considers subjectivity as a fluid and discursive process. Claiming that desire acquires an essence that may be Islamic or secular in nature limits the range of possibilities enabled by the concept of rhizomatic desire.

Viewing desire as productive and not merely confined to secular or religious elements enables a reading of the mutual embeddedness of religion and secularism. Approaching desire from this perspective allows for a more nuanced understanding of the individuals who participate in Islamic movements, as well as global religious movements beyond the persistent construction of "religious subjects" as continuously enacted embodiments of fixed, coherent, and consistent religious practices. Hence, I reject both the polarities in the representation of subjectivity and subject production and the normative binary of the rationality of the secular, public, and political actor versus the irrational, emotional, and private religious self. I explored the disruptions and the consistencies in the ways in which women articulated notions of religiosity, couched in their own histories and contexts to show that these articulations of ritual and religious belief are not isolated from the secular, political processes imbricated in their fabric.

Whether overt or covert, politicized religious discourse is a growing presence across the globe that is gradually occupying a space in modern societies, a fact that challenges secularism theory. Although the impact of this phenomenon is often perceived as countering modernity and as a failure in the modernization process, Talal Asad (2003) contends that proponents of the latter view normalize secularism as an ideology that necessitates the confinement of religion to nonreligious spaces as a contingency for modernity. José Casanova (1994), however, disagrees with Asad. Religious activism, Casanova maintains, is not a threat to secularism. As long as religion is consistent with the principles of modernity, the de-privatization of religion does not undermine secularism. Asad pointed out, however, that only those types of religious activism that are willing to engage liberal parameters are allowed a presence in the public realm, as in the case of France and China.

Asad surmises that political religious activism that voices its concerns and claims its right to express its basic principles cannot have a significant impact on the public domain. The reason, he surmises, is mainly due to the ways that discourse is structured in the public sphere, which not only marginalizes and excludes religious minorities but also fails to provide channels of communication allowing for an exchange of meanings. This discourse is contingent not only on the language that religious groups employ, which by virtue of its religious rhetoric is excluded from secular processes, but also on the listeners' subject production, which structures their reactions and ways of listening to religious discourse.

Faced with the choice of having to secularize their discourses in order to be heard, some of these groups strive to "liberalize" (Kurzman 1998) their traditions, as is evident among Islamic groups in Turkey, Egypt, and Tunisia. The alternative for religious groups to shift gears often is to confront existing assumptions and restricting regimes. Asad reasons that many of these groups may directly challenge the state and threaten its authority and control over the public sphere. The repercussions of such perceived invasions of the public sphere often become violent or coercive practices that threaten personal freedom and create imbalances in the secular system, as exemplified by the Muslim Brotherhood in Egypt, discussed in the first chapter.

What, then, are the implications for women's Islamic activism, and how will their movement be received in Egyptian society if these considerations are taken into account? A few examples from the Middle East illustrate how Islamic activism has fared under the liberal premise of secularization.

Islamic Activism and the Political Process

As in other areas of the world, Middle Eastern politics reflects a complicated, if not messy, context for "democratic" political participation in the public sphere. It excludes the "religious" in some cases because religious groups are equated with "fanaticism" and "irrational extremism." An Enlightenment version of secularism, in which reason and science replace religion, as the basis of public morality has been problematic even in Western countries. In the Middle East, these problems were due largely to a local history that had earlier made attempts at secularization.[5] In addition, secularization has been associated with a colonialist history, opposition to Islam, and indiscriminate support for Western power (Najjar 1996), a view exemplified by almost a century of Western colonization and imperialist agendas. Although secularism is usually seen as liberating the political from the authority of the religious, it was used in Egypt in different contexts to describe a process aimed at marginalizing Islam or excluding it from the restructuring of society during both the colonial and postindependence periods. This situation is further confounded because corrupt ruling classes in the Middle East are seen as the proponents of secularism and are supported by Western powers. In Algeria, the victory of the Islamic Salvation Front (FIS) was violently revoked by the military, backed by secularists and rationalized as means of protecting democracy. Thus, the concept and the application of secularism often contradict its original principles and also threaten the way of life in the Middle East because it is not neutral and is driven not by democratic principles but by extreme power struggles. This explains why, unlike popular belief, in the Middle East today, the Westernized elite are not the proponents of democracy.

Conversely, secularist rule in Tunisia, for instance, presents an alternative case in which marginalized Islamic groups adopt an aggressive program of secularization and modernization. Tunisia's Islamic Tendency Movement (or Renaissance Party), led by Rashid Ghannoushi, initially began as an apolitical cultural group. In 1978 President Habib Bourguiba ordered the military to crush the protestors, and in 1981, Ghannoushi's Islamic Association became a political party known as the MTI (Islamic Tendency Movement), which continues to be severely repressed.

Today, participants in women's Islamic movements in Egypt are not working toward political representation, with the exception of Islamist women like Amany Abul Fadl, who support the Muslim Brotherhood. Women's Islamic activism remains a social reform movement, which, according to the activists of al-Hilal, does not have political aims. In fact, as I have shown in this book, women normalize the distinctions propagated by modernizing projects that claim a private nature for religion as an individual relation to the divine and not as a form of governance. The boundaries between the constructs of the private and public domains of social life are slippery, however. As these women's Islamic movements gain more ground and become even more diverse and widespread, these boundaries may pose a problem for the women activists, as they often have for the Muslim Brotherhood and popular Muslim preachers.

Amr Khaled, a star of Islamic preaching in Egypt is a good example. His attempts to avoid confrontation with the state failed to secure his position in the public sphere, mainly because he became too popular. A similar fate may lie ahead for the women of al-Hilal if the state comes to see their activism as a threat. If this happens, the state will revoke al-Hilal's permits to continue as a private voluntary organization and, consequently, deny it legitimacy as a sanctioned organization. From what I have observed and heard from the women of al-Hilal, they would not accept this without a struggle. They would have to question their assumptions regarding the private nature of Islamic faith, as only then would they see it necessary to use their activism to defy the state and, in doing so, to make it "public."

Islamic women activists in Cairo today negotiate an intricate matrix of relationships and structures. Analyses of this matrix must take account of its interconnectivity, not merely by foregrounding the production of desire through postcolonialist histories of colonialism and nationalism, but also by considering the effects of living in a global world with shifting political priorities and orientations. Islamic women activists come from various socioeconomic, generational, and educational backgrounds. Thus, representing their subjectivities as lodged in religious discourse is too limiting a view, particularly because Islam itself is a discursive tradition, with markers and symbols that shift, change, and acquire new meanings that often merge with or depart from old ones.

The ethnographic data I discussed in this book show that the desires and subjectivities of Islamic women and the nature of their Islamic activism are better understood as historically and culturally mediated by fluid and overlapping secular and religious dimensions. Analyses of secularism and religion in Egypt suggest that women participants in Islamic movements are not caught between the two polarizing forces of a modernizing state and an Islamic return to tradition. Instead, women who participate in Islamic movements normalize these distinctions in their practices. If they perceive religion as separate from politics, they make this distinction within the bounds of law and state politics and not conceptually.

In my interviews with Islamic women activists, I noted that some had difficulty defining religion, and when they did not, they clearly individualized their understanding of it. They almost always place religious practice in the realm of the personal, such as a relationship with God or a spiritual state of being in which one transcends a preoccupation with the material world. Even though their goals and identities are based on an established religious conviction, Islamic women activists also accept secular liberal views that often see the individual as both free and independent but simultaneously acting according to divine will and sovereignty. In contrast, they also displayed their awareness of an interfering state that dominates the public sphere and restricts their role in society to specific areas of social work. Ultimately, all the activist women I talked with maintained that Islam was a way of life that informed everything they did, a sweeping generalization that indiscriminately glossed over the fact that not everything can be Islamically informed, that their way of life is indeed limited to the space that the state affords them, a private and bounded space. While they do participate in public, they clearly feel a need to abide by secular laws and regulations. As they become more deeply involved in Islamic activism, their complex and multifaceted desires mediated by imbricated categories of Islamic religion and secular principles shape their actions and the roles they play in these movements.

My intention in this book was to consider the limitations of normative analytical conceptions that obscure the means by which religion and secularism seamlessly merge in subjecthood and subject production. The bulk of the literature dealing with the categories of the "secular" and the "religious"—as polarizing categories competing for the desires, identities, agency, and selves of women in Islamic societies—obscures the meanings and intentions of these movements. The implications of the critiques discussed here for the interpretation of women's desires and subjectivities may provide opportunities for dialogue and attest to the importance of critically examining systems of representation that draw on normative imperialist and orientalist discourses.

Glossary

al-'almaniyya	secularism
Allah	God
al-thawra	revolution, that is, the 1952 revolution led by the Free Officers
da'iyat	feminine plural of *da'iyah*, literally, one who invites people to the Islamic faith, extended to mean women preachers
da'wah	literally, invitation to Islam
din	religion
doctora	literally, doctor
du'ah	masculine plural of *da'iyah*, literally, one who invites someone to the Islamic faith
dunya	literally, world, the material world
fiqh	Islamic jurisprudence
galabiyya	long, wide garment; Egypt's national dress
gam'iyah	association (singular)
gam'iyat	associations (plural of *gam'iyah*)
hagga	woman who has performed *haj*, pilgrimage
haj	pilgrimage to Mecca
hidayah	guidance
hijab	Islamic headscarf covering a woman's hair; has many styles and forms
ijtihad	independent reasoning
infitah	open door policy, liberalization of the Egyptian economy
kheir	good; *'mal kheir*, good deeds
khimar	headscarf covering the hair and shoulders down to below the waist
li wajhi Allah	literally, for the sake of God, meaning one who does a good act with no other motive than to please God
'mal kheir	good deeds
muhajabbah	woman who wears the *hijab* (see *hijab*)
nashid	religious chant
Qur'an	holy book of Islam

Qur'anic	from the Qur'an, of the Qur'an Rabinah, our God
salafi	someone seeking to return to the unadulterated Islamic practices of the first three generations of the Muslim community
shari'a	Islamic law
shihada	to act as witness; or to witness that there is no God but God and that Muhammad is his prophet; the Islamic declaration of faith
shisha	water pipe common in the Middle East
'ulama	plural of *'alim*, scholar of Islamic teaching
zina	adultery, sexual intercourse outside marriage

Notes

1. To maintain confidentiality, I have changed the names of locations and individuals.

2. The Qur'an is the holy book of Islam. Reciting the Qur'anic text with the proper Arabic enunciation is a technical art form at al-Hilal, where reading lessons emphasize the "correct" pronunciation and intonation.

3. *Gam'iyah* (singular; *gam'iyat*, plural) is an association, like al-Hilal.

4. See Raouf's webpage at www.islamonline.com.

5. In the last few years, women's Islamic activities suffered the brunt of journalistic critique in politically left magazines, which publicly derided and ridiculed their efforts to preach Islamic beliefs. Many of the activist women I have met were initially careful not to volunteer information, for fear that the media would use this against their cause. See Abdel Sami' Gad 2000, 29.

6. While I am aware of the dynamic that prompts critiques of the power that ethnographers wield over their informants in field research, I must say that this was not always the case in my fieldwork with Islamic activist women. In fact, my experiences often revealed that power dynamics were far more complex than they are depicted. For example, I was dealing with informed and well-educated women in regard to the women's Islamic movement in Cairo. To assume that we (anthropologists) are in a position of power denies these subjects their agency.

7. *Da'iyat* is the plural of *da'iyah*, "feminine," which designates a person who invites people to the Islamic faith. Here, this term refers to women who preach and teach in the Islamic movement.

8. The women's Islamic movement in Egypt has various purposes and practices. Here I use the term *Islamic movement* in a general sense to denote the collective action that follows Islamic teachings as a guiding framework for goals and activism.

9. The debate over "Islamic feminism" picked up momentum in February 1994 when, in a lecture at the School of Oriental and African Studies in London, Afsaneh Najmabadi, an Iranian American scholar of gender and history at Harvard University, described a reform movement led by women that joined religious and

secular feminist discourses (Moghadam 2005). Najmabadi focused specifically on Iranian women's activism—both religious and secular—that found an outlet through *Zanan,* a women's magazine. *Zanan's* writers and scholars reinterpreted Islamic texts to reform women's rights in Iran. When women's Islamic movements burgeoned in Muslim-majority countries in the 1990s, observers and scholars of women's issues in the Middle East referred to Najmabadi's specific case of women in Iran—who followed a form of scholarly activism made possible in principle because Iran permits independent reasoning, or *ijtihad*—as a brand of feminism that they saw spreading in the Islamic world.

10. By "modernization," I mean the institutionalization of modern reforms that were implemented in the Muslim world beginning in the nineteenth century in government, legal systems, and social and religious restructuring. In particular, I allude to local cultures and traditions combining with European modernity their productive processes of local debates, selective appropriations, negations, adaptations, and writing. European modernity refers to the ascendancy of science, rationality, and the centralization of the individual as a free, autonomous, bounded, and independent agent.

11. I use secularization here as understood by Talal Asad to mean

> a modern construct based on the legal distinction between public and private, on a political arrangement requiring "religion" to be subjected by law to the private domain, on an ideology of moral individualism and a downgrading of the knowing subject, on a celebration of the physical body as well as on a range of personal sensibilities, that all emerged in Western Europe together with the formation of the modern state. (2001, 1)

Secularization in Egypt developed under particular historical circumstances during the late nineteenth and early twentieth century. According to Asad (2003), the gradual arrival at the separation of "public" and "private" paved the way for the adoption of secular principles. He also cites European colonialism, the influx of Western capital, and the adoption of European contractual laws as factors that made the experience of secular modernity possible in Egypt.

12. Minoo Moallem (1999) departed from the tendency in the literature to see religion/tradition and secularism/modernity as binaries (instead, she focuses on religious fundamentalism). Moallem explains that feminisms and fundamentalisms—specifically Islamic fundamentalisms—are essential components of discourses of modernity, which construct them as two apparently polemic forces and sites of global opposition. Moallem highlights commonalities of feminism and fundamentalism to demonstrate that these oppositional positions are ideological. Salwa Ismail's work (2006) remains a leading example of a contextual approach to examining Islamic activism in Egypt. She asserts that Islamist militant activism merges with forms of local sociality and should not be viewed as marginal groups shunned by popular communities. Instead, she contends that they are part of the social fabric of the urban sphere. Ismail conducts a social, cultural, political, and urban dissection

of the forces that make Islamism possible in Egypt. In addition, the work of Carolyn Rouse (2004) is a very useful study of converts to Islam in the United States. Rouse illustrates the diversity in individuals' religious experience, showing that religious experience is not a uniform, stable process, and she highlights the complex array of social and political processes with which these individuals negotiate.

13. Liberalism is a political, economic, and social ideology that developed around the nineteenth century in Europe and America. In principle, "liberalism" is based on the shrinking role of government vis-à-vis the freedom of individuals and emphasizes individual autonomy, liberty, independence, and choice. Widely disseminated through modern nation-states around the world in the twentieth century, liberal modernity has assumed the proportions of a hegemonic ideology integrated into the so-called nonliberal traditions.

In contrast, I follow Alasdair MacIntyre's reasoning about the liberal tradition: "And so finally modern liberalism, born of antagonism to all tradition, has transformed itself gradually into what is now clearly recognizable even by some of its adherents as one more tradition" (1988, 10). That is, at its inception, the liberal was constructed through opposition to the traditional. In my opinion, while it is possible to speak of a historically nonliberal tradition like "Islam," to make the same distinction for contemporary practice and rationale is highly problematic. Consequently, I propose to taking the discussion of Islamic subjects and desiring processes beyond the liberal/nonliberal research agenda. In this I follow Said's advice to imagine these trajectories by considering why "cultures are hybrid and heterogeneous . . . that cultures and civilizations are so interrelated and interdependent as to beggar any unitary or simply delineated description of their individuality. How can one speak of 'Western civilization' except as in large measure an ideological fiction? (1978, 349).

14. Apart from a number of authors whose work deals with selfhood/subjecthood, I distinguish between the notion of an "essential self" deriving from an essential, absolute, and stable core, and I use "subject" to denote the multiplicity, incompleteness, and seamlessness of a constructed subjecthood.

15. According to Hegel (Russon 2004), desire is the condition of being; the lack of the object of desire perpetuates the desiring self. The self recognizes itself through difference from the other. To Hegel (1966) and also Lacan (1966, 623, 630), lack is associated with desire. Lacan claimed that "le désire est la métonymie du manqué à être" (The lack of the object of desire is the condition for desire). Lacan termed the inability of attainment *un manque d'être*, or a desire to be. The production of desire mirrors the ways in which the subject also is produced through discourses of power. According to Foucault (1979) and Deleuze and Guattari (2004), desire is productive, "desiring consists in interruptions, letting certain flows through, making withdrawals from those flows, cutting the chains that become attached to the flows. . . . Desire does not depend on lack, it's not a lack of something, and it doesn't refer to any law. Desire produces" (Deleuze and Guattari 2004, 232–33).

16. Literally meaning "trodden path" in Islamic teaching, the *sunnah* is the way of the Prophet Muhammad. *Sunnah* relies on the sayings of the Prophet as witnessed by his companions.

17. Codes of Islamic law based on the Qur'an, the example of the Prophet. These codes are *ijma'*, or the consensus of Muslims; *qiyas*, which refers to evidence or example; and finally, *ijtihad*, or independent reasoning. The application of *sharia* as law (*tatbiq al-sharia*) is one of the controversial issues over which Islamists struggle with the state in Egypt.

18. This does not mean however, that women's Islamic activism escapes state ideologies even if they challenge it.

19. Fundamentalist is in quotation marks because what originally described orthodox, conservative groups now denotes extremists and even terrorist Muslim groups.

CHAPTER 2

1. Marx (Marx and Engels 2008) was unrelentingly opposed to religious belief because in his view, it created an illusion of happiness for the oppressed, whose only hope was the awakening of their consciousness. Marx's critique of religion was not merely a personal rejection of it but primarily a critique of society that enables religion to be the "opium of the people." In a similar vein addressing the effect of religious belief on individual consciousness, Freud labeled it an infantile attempt to control an uncontrollable world. He tied religion to human divisiveness and a neurotic tendency to belong to a religious identity that is delusional. More important, Freud regarded religion as irrational and called for a rational analytic to overcome its repressive effects (Freud 1927). Nietzsche regarded Christianity as a religion that evolved into hatred and "one great curse." He maintained that humans do not merely believe in, but created, their gods (Nietzsche 2005).

CHAPTER 3

1. Women are symbols of tradition when they are framed as the transmitters of culture in Islamic discourse. In modernization discourse, however, the same value is seen as negative when tradition is associated with backwardness and stagnation. As symbols of modernization, the role of women as positive contributors in society is emphasized.

2. For an examination of these theories, see Sadowski 1998.

3. Militant forms of Islamism have long since lost momentum in Egypt. Systematically pursued after their assassination of President Sadat in 1981, most militant groups were either in prison or confined to underground cells, from which they periodically resurface to incite isolated incidences of unrest.

4. In an effort to win over public support after the Nasserist period in Egypt, President Sadat not only released a number of Islamists who were imprisoned by

Nasser, but he also compromised on issues of women's rights and family law to gain their favor. The current president, Hosni Mubarak, alternates these political maneuvers with periods of firm policing.

What Hatem does not allude to in her article is the fact that the state also consistently harasses these groups by coercing their consent.

5. The grand mufti is the highest-ranking clerical position in Egypt. He is responsible for arbitration in cases presented to him by the public or the government. He also is in charge of issuing *fatwa*, or religious pronouncements, about cases that require Islamic legal references.

6. The headscarf worn by Muslim women, sometimes including a *niqab*, a veil that covers the face except for the eyes.

7. *Al-Masry al-Yom* is the leading opposition newspaper in Egypt, publishing the writings of various analysts who express these views. Foremost among these analysts are Hassan Nafaa, Nasr Hamid Abu Zeid, Amr al-Shoubky, and Amr Hamazawy.

8. Islamic Center for Study and Research, *The Muslim Woman in Muslim Society* (*Al-shourah wa ta'adod al-ahazab*), 1994. The first sentence in the booklet on women in Muslim society reads as follows: "A woman is a mother whom the Qur'an mentioned as having heaven under her feet. . . . And a woman is a daughter and a sister who is born like her male brother from the same "*solb*" [source] and womb. . . . And a woman is the wife, a home for her husband as he is a home for her" (1).

9. I do not view these historical themes as bounded or linear periods. These are intertwined events that do not necessarily end and begin as exactly as the dates suggest. These dates are merely a guide. Many of the themes have far-reaching effects, as I pointed out earlier.

10. Sadat's open door policy was designed to bring international capital to Egypt.

11. Scholars of Islamic studies.

12. Mitchell (1988, 69). According to Mitchell, Ibrahim Adham established the model school in 1843.

13. Islamic elementary schools where instruction is based on the Qur'an.

14. A *salafi* Muslim is literally an "early Muslim," a term alluding to the early centuries of Islamic practice. Salafia is a modern movement in Islam that regards contemporary Islamic interpretation as corrupt and seeks to return to an unadulterated Islamic practice of the first three generations of the Muslim community. It is often translated as "fundamentalist Islamic practice," but it does not necessarily mean that *salafi* Muslims are extremists. There is, of course, a wide range of followers of *salafi* Islam.

15. The British colonial administration was interested only in primary education and did not encourage secondary education. In fact, the British administration staunchly opposed higher education (Ahmed 1992).

16. Mitchell (1991, 99). Shakry (1998) also makes a similar point in regard to European and Islamic notions of discipline.

17. Independent reasoning.

18. "The Arabic term for secularism is *'almaniyya*. According to the Arabic Language Academy in Cairo, the term is derived from *'alam* (world), and not from *'ilm* (science), as some people think, thus giving the wrong impression that science is opposed to religion. Some writers use the Arabic term *'alamaniyya* in order to avoid confusion. Others prefer *dunyawiyya* (worldly), in contrast to *dini* (religious). In Coptic liturgy, the term *'almaniyyun* is used to connote laymen (most of the members of the congregation) who do not belong to the clergy class." See Fauzi Najjar, "The Debate on Islam and Secularism in Egypt," *Arab Studies Quarterly* (Spring): 4–6.

19. For a review of this literature, see Hafez (2003).

20. I follow Najib Ghadbian: "'Islamist' denotes *Islamiyyun*, [which] is what people belonging to Islamist movements call themselves. . . . The majority of the Arab world is Muslim, while only those with ideologies that call for the implementation of Islam in the public as well as private realms are Islamists" (1997, 7).

21. Invitation to Islamic faith, to spread the word of Islam.

22. Those who have challenged this tendency include Altorki and Nelson.

CHAPTER 4

1. According to the National Council for Women, female-headed households comprised 16 percent of all Egyptian households in 2000.

2. *Fiqh* is Islamic jurisprudence; *shari'a* is Islamic law.

3. This fact is significant, since studies have shown that since the turn of the twentieth century, the middle class in Egypt has been the target of modernizing processes seeking to create new subjects of a secular state.

4. *Da'wa* is an invitation to the Islamic faith.

5. State-owned newspapers such as *Al-Ahram* ignore these women's efforts, and *Al-Masry al-Youm*, an independent newspaper in Egypt, is often opposed to Islamic activism of any kind. In the 1990s, the left-wing Egyptian magazine *Rose El Youssef* began slandering the women's Islamic movements, calling the new women preachers misguided and "empty-headed." See *Rose El Youssef* 3750 (2000): 24–29.

6. There is no shyness in religion, meaning there are no subjects that cannot be discussed in Islam because they are shameful or embarrassing.

7. This is an expression meaning consensual extramarital intercourse.

8. Do we apply Islamic punishment (*hadd*)? According to the Qur'an (sura 24, vv. 2–2), four eyewitnesses are required to be convicted of *zina*. In most Islamic schools, pregnancy, for example, is not considered sufficient evidence of *zina*.

9. For her discussion of "scientific mothering," see Shakry 1998.

10. Pilgrimage to Mecca, one of the five pillars of Islam.

11. A colloquial term describing a veiled woman. In *fushah* (classic) Arabic, *muhajabah* would be used. The "g" is the colloquial equivalent of the "j" in *fushah*. Because we were having a conversation, as opposed to a religious lesson, Dalia was using the informal term.

12. Sufism is a body of beliefs with different meanings in different contexts. A very general understanding would denote Sufism as a "mystic tradition." But it can be argued that Islamic tradition in its totality relies also on an element of mysticism, the duality of body and spirit.

13. A term derived from *hoda*, "to become enlightened in Islam."

14. I continue to distinguish between modern notions of an "essential self" and the "subject" in its multiple, incomplete constructedness.

15. This was the motto of the 1919 nationalist revolution, which then was adopted by the Wafd Party and is used in Islamic activist women's rhetoric and ideals. The redeployment of this motto reflects al-Hilal's somewhat private view of religion.

16. This is a saying by the Prophet Muhammad: *La darar wala dirar fi al-Islam*, meaning "No injury should be imposed, nor an injury be inflicted, as a penalty for another injury."

17. Al-Salafia communities are varied and diverse, although they have their own vision of how the first three generations of Muslims practiced Islam as a way of living a pure version of the religion.

CHAPTER 5

1. According to Ibn Abidin, a Hanafi scholar and jurist, there are three requirements for intention: (1) Resolution: the minimum legally valid intention to resolve to perform an action; (2) Reward: the intention to draw closer to Allah; and (3) Time: the intention made as or just before one initiates the action. Ibn Abidin then explained, "Worshipping Allah exclusively is obligatory and showing off one's good works (*riya'*), which is to desire something from them other than Allah, is prohibited by scholarly consensus (Arabic: *ijma'*), according to the texts on this. The Prophet (Allah bless him and give him peace) called showing off in good works (*riya'*) the lesser transgression (polytheism). This intention [of drawing closer to Allah] is for achieving reward, not merely validity, for validity related to fulfilling the conditions (*shurut*) and performing the integrals (*arkan*) and the intention related to validity mean knowing in one's heart which prayer one is performing" (Ibn Abidin 1987).

2. This applies to action performed strictly for God's favor.

3. The general meaning is that whatever you do is determined by *niyya* (intention). Each intention has consequences.

4. This word means, literally, "our lord."

5. Alexandria is a beach town on the northern shores of Egypt overlooking the Mediterranean.

6. Transactions, as opposed to *'ibadat*, which pertain to Islamic ritual and worship.

CHAPTER 6

1. By mediated subjectivity, I am referring to the notion of human subjectivity projected onto the attributes of a monotheistic deity—attributes such as omnipotence, omniscience, and volition—and then partially reappropriated by humans. In this scheme, human subjectivity is contingent on God's subjectivity. Thus while human subjectivity is not denied, it is never independent of God's subjectivity, so in this sense, it is "mediated."

Although the idea of mediated subjectivity merits a deeper examination than this book can offer, I find its use in interpreting the kind of contractual relationship I observed at Mehmeit to be helpful. The contractual agreement I observed between the village women of Mehmeit and the activists of al-Hilal leaned more toward a labor agreement that, despite the project's overall Islamic character, viewed individuals as autonomous and free contractual beings and not as subjects mediated by divine will. I might see a mediated subjectivity in the relationship between the activists and divine will.

2. A long Egyptian garment worn by both men and women.

3. A water tobacco pipe.

4. The Qur'anic *sura* (verse) that begins the Qur'an, Islam's holy book. Muslims often recite the *fatha* before embarking on a project, in marriage ceremonies, over loved ones who have died, in prayer, and, today, when they are about to start work.

5. Most of the villagers use the term *doctora* for people from urban areas who fit their profile of an educated person. It does not necessarily mean that these persons have a doctorate or a medical degree. In my view, this term indicates the change in perception of rural communities toward those city dwellers. Being educated is a sign of prestige in the village. Rank is no longer determined by social class alone, but by individual achievement and the *shihada*, a certificate from the Ministry of Education. This is a direct impact of the goals of al-Thawra, the revolution of 1952 that offered free public education to all social classes. The current decline in these services is due to the lack of strategic planning for sustaining these services to a growing population of 80 million, up from 22 million in the 1950s when these changes were made. My statistics are from Anne Goujon, Huda Alkitkat, Wolfgang Lutz, and Isolde Prommer for the Population and Human Capital in Egypt Project carried out by the IIASA in collaboration with the Cairo Demographic Center at the Academy of Scientific Research and Technology (ASRT) on March 7, 2007.

6. To Arabic speakers, Masr means Egypt. Villagers call Cairo Masr because it is the administrative and economic center of the country and also because it indicates the centralization of power in Egypt. In villagers' eyes, Cairo is synonymous with the entire country, making rural areas all the more insignificant in comparison. I have never, to this day, heard anyone use the word al-Qahira, the original Arab-Islamic name of the city.

7. Certificate of education.

8. Literally, my life partner.

CHAPTER 7

1. A type of veil that shows the face and covers the shoulders and arms to the waist.

2. According to UN Development Program, 97 percent of Egyptian women between the ages of fifteen and forty-nine undergo female circumcision.

3. Omaima Abou Bakr is an associate professor in Cairo University's English department.

4. The plural of *da'iyah,* meaning one who invites Islam into a person's life.

5. The well-known history of the Mutazalites of the eighth century and the four-hundred-year debates with the Asharites about the rationality of Islamic religious belief led to the former's rejection of a state system based on religious law, or *shari'a.* For more on the schismic debates between the Mutazalites and the Asharites, see Rahman 2000.

Bibliography

Abdel Kader, Soha. 1987. *Egyptian Women in a Changing Society, 1899–1987*. Boulder, CO: Lynne Rienner.

Abdel Raziq, Ali. 1978. *Al-Islam wa usul al-hukm: Bahth fi-l khilafa wa-l hukuma fi-l Islam* (*Islam and the Foundations of Governance: Research on the Caliphate and Governance in Islam*). Critique and commentary by Mamdooh Haqqi. Beirut.

Abdel Sami' Gad, Mohamed. 2000. "Today's Fad That All Who 'Stand and Stamp' [Their Feet] Discuss Politics, Religion and Sex." *Rose el Youssef* 3751: 29.

Abou Bakr, Omaima. 2001. "Islamic Feminism? What's in a Name?" *Middle East Women's Studies Review* 15, no. 16 (winter/spring): 1–4.

Abu-Lughod, Lila. 1998. "The Marriage of Feminism and Islamism in Egypt: Selective Repudiation as a Dynamic of Postcolonial Cultural Politics." In *Remaking Women: Feminism and Modernity in the Middle East*, ed. Lila Abu-Lughod, 243–69. Princeton, NJ: Princeton University Press.

———. 2004. *Dramas of Nationhood: The Politics of Television in Egypt*. Cairo: American University in Cairo Press.

Adeeb, Monir, and Yousry Ebeed. 2009. "The Brothers Escalate Their Attacks against the Nationalist Party . . . and Criticize Their Ostracization from the *Hiwar*." *Al-Masry al-Yom*, June 11.

Ahmed, Leila. 1992. *Women and Gender in Islam*. New Haven, CT: Yale University Press.

Ali, Nadje Sadig al-. 2000. *Secularism, Gender and the State in the Middle East: The Egyptian Women's Movement*. Cambridge: Cambridge University Press.

Amin, Galal. 1997. *Matha hadath lil Masreen?* (*Whatever Has Happened to the Egyptians?*). Cairo: Dar el Hilal.

Amin, Qasim. 2000. *The Liberation of Women: Two Documents in the History of Egyptian Feminism*. Trans. Samiha Sidhom Peterson. Cairo: American University in Cairo Press.

Anzaldua, Gloria. 1994. "Borderlands / La Frontera: Cultural Studies, 'Difference,' and the Non-Unitary Subject." *Cultural Critique* 28: 5–28.

Asad, Talal. 1973. *Anthropology and the Colonial Encounter*. Atlantic Highlands, NJ: Humanities Press.

———. 1993. *Genealogies of Religion: Discipline and Reasons of Power in Christianity and Islam*. Baltimore: Johns Hopkins University Press.

———. 1996. "Modern Power and the Reconfiguration of Religious Traditions." *SEHR*, February 27.

———. 2001. "Thinking about Secularism and Law in Egypt." *ISIM* 2: 1–15.

———. 2003. *Formations of the Secular: Christianity, Islam, Modernity.* Palo Alto, CA: Stanford University Press.

Ashcroft, Bill, Gareth Griffiths, and Helen Tiffin. 2003. *The Post-Colonial Studies Reader.* London: Arnold.

Badran, Margot. 1991. "Competing Agenda: Feminists, Islam and the State in Nineteenth and Twentieth-Century Egypt." In *Women, Islam, and the State*, ed. Deniz Kandiyoti, 201–36. Philadelphia: Temple University Press.

———. 1996. *Feminists, Islam, and Nation: Gender and the Making of Modern Egypt.* Cairo: American University in Cairo Press.

Bardini, Shaymaa al-, and Hamdy Dabsh. 2009. "Masrahiyya islamiyya dun nisaa aw aghany ʿala masrah Nada thalith ayyam al-ʿyd" (An Islamic Play without Women at the Nada Theater the Third Day of Bairam). *Al-Masry al-Youm* 3, no. 921 (December 31).

Baron, Beth. 2005. *Egypt as a Woman: Nationalism, Gender, and Politics.* Berkeley: University of California Press.

Berger, Peter. 2001. "Reflections on the Sociology of Religion Today." *Sociology of Religion* 62 (winter): 443–54.

Bhabha, H. K. 1996. "Cultures in Between." In *Questions of Cultural Identity*, ed. S. Hall and P. Du Gay, 53–60. London: Sage.

Botman, Selma. 1999. *Engendering Citizenship in Egypt.* New York: Columbia University Press.

Bowen, John. 1998. *Religion in Culture and Society.* Boston: Allyn & Bacon.

Braidotti, R. 1987. *Subjects of Desire: Hegelian Reflections in Twentieth-Century France.* New York: Columbia University Press.

———. 1994. *Nomadic Subjects: Embodiment and Sexual Difference in Contemporary Feminist Theory.* New York: Columbia University Press.

Butler, Judith. 1987. *Subjects of Desire: Hegelian Reflections in Twentieth-Century France.* New York: Columbia University Press.

———. 1993. *Bodies That Matter: On the Discursive Limits of "Sex."* New York: Routledge.

Casanova, José. 1994. *Public Religions in the Modern World.* Chicago: University of Chicago Press.

Chakrabarty, Dipesh. 1992. "Postcoloniality and the Artifice of History: Who Speaks for 'Indian' Pasts?" *Representations* 37 (winter): 1–26.

Chinoy, Shahnaz Taplin. 2006. "A Veil of Uncertainty: While Some Arab Women Embrace the Rise of Islamist Political Parties, Others Fear They Could End Up Groaning under Taliban-Like Regimes." *Salon.com*, June 17. Available at http://www.salon.com/news/feature/2006/06/13/arab_women/.

Clifford, James. 1988. *The Predicament of Culture: Twentieth-Century Ethnography. Literature, and Art.* Cambridge, MA: Harvard University Press.

Cole, Juan Ricardo. 1981. "Feminism, Class, and Islam in Turn of the Century Egypt." *International Journal of Middle East Studies* 13: 387– 407.

Coleman, Daniel. 1998. *Masculine Migrations: Reading the Postcolonial Male In "New Canadian" Narratives*. Toronto: University of Toronto Press.

Comaroff, Jean, and John Comaroff. 1991. *Of Revelation and Revolution*. Chicago: University of Chicago Press.

Cooke, Miriam. 2001. *Women Claim Islam: Creating Islamic Feminism through Literature*. New York: Routledge.

Daugherty, Mary Lee. 1999. "Serpent Handlers: When the Sacrament Comes Alive." In *Christianity in Appalachia: Profiles in Regional Pluralism*, ed. B. Leonard, 138–52. Knoxville: University of Tennessee Press.

Deeb, Lara. 2006. *An Enchanted Modern: Gender and Public Piety in Shi'i Lebanon*. Princeton, NJ: Princeton University Press.

Deleuze, Gilles. 1988. *Foucault*. Trans. Seán Hand. Minneapolis: University of Minnesota Press.

Deleuze, Gilles, and Félix Guattari. 1983. *Anti-Oedipus*. Trans. Robert Hurley, Mark Seem, and Helen R. Lane. Minneapolis: University of Minnesota Press.

———. 2004. *A Thousand Plateaus: Capitalism and Schizophrenia*. Trans. Mark Seem and Helen R. Lane. Minneapolis: University of Minnesota Press.

Dobbelaere, K. 1981. "Secularization: A Multi-dimensional Concept." *Current Sociology* 29: 1–213.

Durkheim, Émile. 1954. *The Elementary Forms of Religious Life*. New York: Free Press.

Eickelman, Dale. 1985. *Knowledge and Power in Morocco: The Education of a Twentieth-Century Notable*. Princeton, NJ: Princeton University Press.

Esposito, John. 1992. *The Islamic Threat: Myth or Reality?* New York: Oxford University Press.

Ewing, Katherine Pratt. 1990. "The Illusion of Wholeness: 'Culture,' 'Self,' and the Experience of Inconsistency." *Ethos* 18, no. 3: 251–78.

———. 1997. *Arguing Sainthood: Islam, Modernity and Psychoanalysis*. Durham, NC: Duke University Press.

Fanon, Frantz. 1967. *Black Skin, White Masks*. London: Pluto Press.

Fernandez, James W. 1986. "The Argument of Images and the Experience of Returning to the Whole." In *The Anthology of Experience*, ed. V. W. Turner and E. M. Bruner, 159–87. Urbana-Champaign: University of Illinois Press.

Fernea, Elizabeth. 1998. *In Search of Islamic Feminism: One Woman's Global Journey*. New York: Doubleday.

———. 2000. "The Challenges for Middle Eastern Women in the 21st Century." *Middle East Journal* 54, no. 2 (spring): 185–93.

Foucault, Michel. 1977. *Discipline and Punish: The Birth of the Prison*. London: Allen Lane.

———. 1979. *The History of Sexuality*. Vol. 1, *An Introduction*. New York: Vintage Books.

———. 1980. *Power/Knowledge: Selected Interviews and Other Writings, 1972–1977*, ed. Colin Gordon. New York: Harvester Wheatsheaf.

Freud, Sigmund. 1927. *The Future of an Illusion*. In *The Standard Edition*, vol. 21. Trans. James Strachney. New York: Norton.

Geertz, Clifford. 1975. *The Interpretation of Cultures*. London: Hutchinson.

———. 1986. *Islam Observed: Religious Development in Morocco and Indonesia*. Chicago: University of Chicago Press.

Ghadbian, Najib. 1997. *Democratization and the Islamist Challenge in the Arab World*. Boulder, CO: Westview Press.

Ghazali, Abdel-Hamid al-. 1994. *Man Is the Basis of the Islamic Strategy for Economic Development*. Islamic Economics Translation Series 1. Jidda: Islamic Research and Training Institute.

Ghazali, Zeinab al-. 1982. *Ayyam min hayaty* (*Days of My Life*). Cairo: Dar al-Shuruq.

Gittings, Clare, and Peter Jupp, eds. 1999. *Death in England*. Manchester: Manchester University Press.

Goël, Nilufer. 1996. *The Forbidden Modern: Civilization and Veiling*. Ann Arbor: University of Michigan Press.

Goujon, Anne, Huda Alkitkat, Wolfgang Lutz, and Isolde Prommer. 2007. *Population and Human Capital in Egypt*. Project by IIASA in collaboration with the Cairo Demographic Center, Academy of Scientific Research and Technology (ASRT). Presented at the Workshop on Population, Human Capital and Water in Egypt, Cairo, March 7.

Guenena, Nemat. 1986. *The "Jihad": An Islamic Alternative in Egypt*. Cairo Papers in Social Science 9. Cairo: American University in Cairo Press.

Guindi, Fadwa el-. 1999a. "Veiling Resistance." *Fashion Theory* 3, no. 1: 51–80.

———. 1999b. *Veil: Modesty, Privacy and Resistance*. New York: Berg.

Haddad, Yvonne Yazbeck, and John L. Esposito. *Islam, Gender, and Social Change*. 1998. Oxford: Oxford University Press.

Haenni, Patrick, and Husam Tammam. 2003. "Egypt's Air-Conditioned Islam." *Le Monde diplomatique*, September. Available at http://mondediplo.com/2003/09/03egyptislam.

Hafez, Sherine. 2003. *The Terms of Empowerment: Islamic Women Activists in Egypt*. Cairo Papers in Social Science 24. Cairo: American University in Cairo Press.

Hatem, Mervat. 1986. "The Enduring Alliance of Nationalism and Patriarchy in Muslim." *Feminist Issues* 6: 19–43.

———. 1992. "Economic and Political Liberation in Egypt and the Demise of State Feminism." *International Journal of Middle East Studies* 24: 231–51.

———. 1998. "Secular and Islamist Discourses on Modernity in Egypt and Evolution of the Postcolonial Nation-State." In *Islam, Gender, and Social Change*, ed. Yvonne Yazbeck Haddad and John L. Esposito, 85–99. Oxford: Oxford University Press.

Hegel, G. W. F. 1966. *The Phenomenology of Mind*. New York: Humanities Press.

Hoodfar, Homa. 2001. "The Veil in Their Minds and on Our Heads: Veiling Practices and Muslim Women in the Politics and Culture in the Shadow of the Capital." In *Women, Gender and Religion*, ed. Elizabeth Anne Castelli and Rosamond C. Rodman, 440–46. New York: Palgrave Macmillan.

Ibn Adbin, Mohamed Amin Ben 'Omar Abdin (A. H. 1252/1852). 1987. *Radd al-Mokhtar'ala al-Dory al-Mukhtar*. Cairo: Bulaq Edition. Repr., Beirut: Dar Ihya' al-Turath al-'Arabi.

———. 1996. "The Debate on Islam and Secularism in Egypt." *Arab Studies Quarterly*, March 22: 48–51.

Imara, Mohamed. 1991. "Nazariyyat al-Hakimiyya fi Fikr Abi al-'A'la al-Mawdudi." In *Ishkaliyyat al-Fikr al-Islami al-Mu'asir*, ed. Fauzi Najjar, 139–57. Valletta: Islamic World Studies Centre.

Islamic Center for Study and Research. 1994. *Al-Shourah wa ta'adod al-ahazab* (*The Muslim Woman in the Muslim Society*). Cairo: Islamic Center for Study and Research, 1994.

Ismail, Salwa. 2006. *Rethinking Islamist Politics: Culture, the State and Islamism*. London: I. B. Taurus.

James, William. 1979. *The Varieties of Religious Experience*. Charlottesville: University of Virginia Library, Electronic Text Center.

Jansen, Wilhelmina. 1998. "Contested Identities: Women and Religion in Algeria and Jordan." In *Women and Islamization: Contemporary Dimensions of Discourse on Gender Relations*, ed. Karin Ask and Marit Tjomsland, 73–102. New York: Berg.

Joseph, Suad. 1996. "Gender and Citizenship in Middle East States." *Middle East Report*, January/March, 4–10.

———. 2005. "Relational Pedagogies and the Desiring Female Subject in Lebanon in Press." *Journal of Middle East Women's Studies* 1, no. 1: 79–109.

Juergensmeyer, Mark. 2001. "The Global Rise of Religious Nationalism." In *Religions/Globalizations: Theories and Cases*, ed. Dwight Hopkins, 66–83. Durham, NC: Duke University Press.

Kandil, Amany, and Sara Ben Nafiss. 1992. *Al-jam'eyyat al-ahliyyah fi Misr* (*Citizens' Societies in Egypt*). Cairo: MDSE.

Kandiyoti, D. 1996. "Contemporary Feminist Scholarship and Middle East Studies." In *Gendering the Middle East: Gender, Culture, and Politics in the Middle East*, ed. L. Ahmed, M. Cook, and S. Sharoni, 1–28. Syracuse, NY: Syracuse University Press.

Karam, Azza. 1998. *Women, Islamism and the State: Contemporary Feminism in Egypt*. New York: Macmillan.

Khan, Shahnaz. 2002. *Aversion and Desire: Negotiating Muslim Female Identity in the Diaspora*. Toronto: Women's Press.

Kipnis, Andrew. 2001. "The Flourishing of Religion in Post-Mao China and the Anthropological Category of Religion." *Australian Journal of Anthropology* 12, no. 1: 32–46.

Krauss, Wolfgang. 2000. "Timely Stories: Narrating a Self in Postmodern Times." Paper presented at the First International Conference on the Dialogical Self, Nijmegen, Netherlands, June 23–26.

Kurzman, Charles. 1998. *Liberal Islam: A Sourcebook*. New York: Oxford University Press.

Lacan, Jacques. *Écrits*. Paris: Seuil, 1966.

Lazreg, Marnia. 1994. *The Eloquence of Silence: Algerian Women in Question*. New York: Routledge.

Luhmann, Niklas. 1990. *Essays on Self-Reference*. New York: Columbia University Press.

MacIntyre, A. 1988. *Whose Justice? Which Rationality?* South Bend, IN: University of Notre Dame Press.

Mahmood, Saba. 2001. "Feminist Theory, Embodiment, and the Docile Agent: Some Reflections on the Egyptian Islamic Revival." *Cultural Anthropology* 6, no. 2: 202–36.

———. 2005. *The Politics of Piety: The Islamic Revival and the Feminist Subject*. Princeton, NJ: Princeton University Press.

Malinowski, Bronislaw. 1922. *Argonauts of the Western Pacific*. New York: Dutton.

———. 1948. *Magic, Science and Religion, and Other Essays*. Boston: Beacon Press.

Marx, Karl, and Friedrich Engels. 2008. *On Religion*. New York: Dover.

Merleau-Ponty, Maurice. 2002. *Phenomenology of Perception*. London: Routledge Classics.

Mernissi, Fatima. 1991. *The Veil and the Male Elite: A Feminist Interpretation of Women's Rights in Islam*. New York: Basic Books.

Mitchell, Timothy. 1988. *Colonizing Egypt*. New York: Cambridge University Press.

———. 1991. "The Limits of the State: Beyond Statist Approaches and Their Critics." *American Political Science Review* 85, no. 1: 77–96.

Moallem, Minoo. 1999. "Transnationalism, Feminism, and Fundamentalism." In *Between Woman and Nation: Nationalisms, Transnational Feminisms and the State*, ed. Caren Kaplan, Norma Alarcon, and Minoo Moallem, 320–48. Durham, NC: Duke University Press.

Moghadam, V. M. 2005. "Islamic Feminism: Its Discontents and Its Prospects." Paper presented at the First International Congress on Islamic Feminism, Barcelona, October 27–29. Available at http://www.feminismeislamic.org/eng/.

Moghissi, Haideh. 1999. *Feminism and Islamic Fundamentalism: The Limits of Postmodern Analysis*. London: Zed Books.

Mohanty, Chandra Talpade. 1988. "Under Western Eyes: Feminist Scholarship and Colonial Discourses." *Feminist Review* 30: 65–88.

Mojab, Shahrazad. 2001. "Theorizing The Politics of 'Islamic Feminism.'" *Feminist Review* 69: 124–46.

Morris, Brian. 1998. *Anthropological Studies of Religion: An Introductory Text*. Cambridge: Cambridge University Press.

Nafaa, Hassan. 2006. "Al-Ikhwan wa'l dawla wa'l indifaa' al-sari' nahw al-hawiya" (The Brotherhood and the State: Rapid Acceleration toward the Edge). *Al-Masry al-Youm*, December 17, 13.

Najjar, Fauzi. 1996. "The Debate on Islam and Secularism in Egypt." *Arab Studies Quarterly* (spring): 4–6.

Nelson, Cynthia. 1986. "The Voices of Doria Shafik: Feminist Consciousness in Egypt from 1940–1960." *Feminist Issues* 6, no. 2: 15–31.

Nietzsche, Friedrich. 2005. *The Anti-Christ.* Trans. H. L. Mencken. London: Cosimo Books.

Ong, Aiwa. 1990. "State Versus Islam: Malay Families, Women's Bodies, and the Body Politic in Malaysia." *American Ethnologist* 17: 258–76.

Özyürek, Esra. 2006. *Nostalgia for the Modern: State Secularism and Everyday Politics in Turkey.* Durham, NC: Duke University Press.

Pateman, Carol. 1988. *The Sexual Contract.* Oxford: Polity Press.

Rabinow, Paul. 1986. "Representations Are Social Facts: Modernity and Post-Modernity in Anthropology." In *Writing Culture: The Poetics and Politics of Ethnography*, ed. James Clifford and George E. Marcus, 234–61. Berkeley: University of California Press.

Rahman, Fazlur. 2000. *Revival and Reform in Islam.* Oxford: One World.

Rapport, N., and J. Overing. 2000. *Social and Cultural Anthropology: The Key Concepts.* London: Routledge.

Rasmussen, Lene Current. 2004. "Higab and the Education of Self." *Issues in Comparative Education* 7, no. 1: 70–79.

Robbins, L. 1961. *The Theory of Economic Policy in English Classical Political Economy.* London: Macmillan.

Rouse, Carolyn. 2004. *Engaged Surrender: African American Women and Islam.* Berkeley: University of California Press.

Russon, John Edward. 2004. *Reading Hegel's Phenomenology.* Bloomington: Indiana University Press.

Sadda, Hoda el-. 1999. "Remembering Aisha Taymour (1840–1902)." Paper presented at the WMF Conference, Cairo.

Sadowski, Yahya. 1998. *The Myth of Global Chaos.* Washington, DC: Brookings Institution Press.

Said, Edward. W. 1978. *Orientalism.* New York: Pantheon.

Sayyid-Marsot, Afaf Lutfi. 1995. *Women and Men in Late Eighteenth-Century Egypt.* Austin: University of Texas Press.

Shahidian, Hammed. 2002. *Women in Iran: Emerging Voices in the Women's Movement.* Westport, CT: Greenwood Press.

Shakry, Omnia. 1998. "Schooled Mothers and Structured Play: Child Rearing in Turn-of-the-Century Egypt." In *Remaking Women: Feminism and Modernity in the Middle East*, ed. Lila Abu-Lughod, 126–70. Princeton, NJ: Princeton University Press.

Spivak, Gayatri. 1988. "Can the Subaltern Speak?" In *Marxism and the Interpretation of Culture*, ed. Cary Nelson and Lawrence Grossberg, 271–313. Urbana-Champaign: University of Illinois Press.

———. 2005. "Scattered Speculations on the Subaltern and the Popular." *Postcolonial Studies* 8, no. 4: 475–86.

Starrett, Gregory. 1998. *Putting Islam to Work*. Berkeley: University of California Press.

Stoler, Ann Laura. 1995. *Race and the Education of Desire: Foucault's History of Sexuality and the Colonial Order of Things*. Durham, NC: Duke University Press.

Talhami, Hashem Ghada. 1996. *The Mobilization of Muslim Women in Egypt*. Gainsville: University Press of Florida.

Tylor, Edward Burnett. 1958. *Religion in Primitive Culture*. New York: Harper Bros.

Vahdat, Farzin. 2003. "Critical Theory and the Islamic Encounter with Modernity." In *Islam and the West: Critical Perspectives on Modernity*, ed. Michael J. Thomson, 123–38. Lanham, MD: Rowman & Littlefield.

Voyé, Lillian. 1999. "Secularization in a Context of Advanced Modernity." *Sociology of Religion* 60, no. 3: 275–88.

Wagner, Peter. 1994. *A Sociology of Modernity: Liberty and Discipline*. London: Routledge.

Weber, Max. 1958. *The Social Psychology of the World-Religions*. In *From Max Weber: Essays in Sociology*, ed. H. H. Gerth and C. Wright Mills. New York: Oxford University Press.

———. 1963. *The Sociology of Religion*. Trans. Ephraim Fischoff. Boston: Beacon Press.

Weedon, C. 1987. *Feminist Practice and Poststructuralist Theory*. Oxford: Blackwell.

World Bank. 2002. *Arab Republic of Egypt. Poverty Reduction in Egypt: Diagnosis and Strategies*. Washington, DC: World Bank.

Young, Robert. 1995. *Colonial Desire: Hybridity in Culture, Theory and Race*. New York: Routledge.

Yunis, Mona. 1993. *Wagh bala makyadj (A Face without Makeup)*. Cairo: Dar el-Tauzi`a wa al-Nashar al-Islamiyya.

Index

'almaniyya, 170

Abdel-Nasser, Gamal, 65; and the Muslim Brotherhood, 68

Abdel-Raziq, Ali, 63

Abduh, Muhammad, 63

Abu-Lughod, Lila, 6; analysis of Qasim Amin, 64; dramas of nationhood, 6

Abul Fadl, Amany, 151; and state policing 152; views and activism, 153

Agency, 9–11; autonomous agency, 103; inconsistency of, 11; liberal definition, 10; Mahmood's critique, 11

Ahmed, Labiba, 66–67, 70

Ahmed, Leila, 11, 61; critique of Qasim Amin, 64, 65

Al-'adawiyya, Rab'a, 90, 89

Al-Azhar University, 54, 63, 68, 119, 152

Al-Banna, Hassan, 67

al da'wa, 83; training, 109, 163, 170n4

Al-Ghazali, Zeinab, 67–68, 69, 130

Al-Hilal, 1, 19; activism, 80–81; and education, 83, 93, 98–99, 103; rural social reform, 138–148

Al Wafd, 64; secularism, 66, 171n15

al-zy al-islamy, 73

Amin, Qasim, 63; critiques of, 64; and modern liberal discourse, 64

Arabic, 20; classic, 171n11; command of, 122, 125, 137; enunciation, 2, 165n2; fluency and authenticity, 66, 61; and Qur'an 139; schools, 108, 111

Arborescent thought, 103

Asad, Talal. 40; and Geertz, 40–41; hybridity, 104; religious activism and public discourse, 66; on secularization, 166n11

Autonomy, 11, 14, 20, 34, 78, 96, 103, 115, 132, 133, 158

Binaries, 28, 38, 66; in critique of subjectivity, 27, 57; Islam and modernity, 9; non-binarizing approaches, 8; in Orientalist thought, 33, 50; in religious activism, 60, 154, 156; religious movements and the state, 46; secular and religious feminists 153; secular/religious binary, 46, 79; as a technique of conversion, 92

Cairo, 20, 52, 134, 144, 145; American university, 122; Arabic language academy, 170n18; Islamic activism, 7, 77; Islamization 73; local infrastructure 73; PVO networks, 81, 83, 148; suburbs, 72, 80, 84; tourist sites, 120; transportation, 137; university, 1, 44, 81, 108, 115, 119, 129; women's movements, 24, 58, 82, 85, 91, 93

China: case study, 28; Falun Gong, 47; religious movements, 46, 47, 158

Civic community, 121

Class(es) 62, 83, 149; clergy, 170; educated, 149, 172; elites, 61; and funerary practices, 107; lower, 61, 63, 67, 71, 87, 106, 118; middle class, 22, 67, 71, 82, 83, 117;

Class(es) (*continued*): and modernization, 170n3; Qasim Amin upper class
bias, 64; ruling, 30; upper, 62, 63;
upper middle, 118, 122; and village
life, 172n5; and women's activism, 7,
82; and women's labor outside the
home, 86

Colonialism, 11; and anthropology, 32;
British, 56; and disciplinary techniques, 56; and educational systems
after independence, 56; Foucault, 13;
and fragmentation and hybridity,
21; French, in Algeria, 156; ; in India
and Egypt, 15; and the production
of desire, 4, 17; and secularization,
166; and veiling practices, 11; and
Westernization, 65

Contractual relationships, 132, 141, 148;
European laws, 166; as opposed to
mediated subjectivity, 172n1

da'iyat 2, 85, 111, 119, 155, 163, 165; and
da'wa, 110–111; Shereen Fathi, 84–85

Death, 37, 68, 111; funeral practices
Egypt, 106–108; in liberal secular
traditions, 107; as regulating the
population in Egypt, 125, 152

Deeb, Lara, and "the enchanted
modern," 7, 9

Deleuze, Gilles (and Felix Guattari), 5,
102–104; and desire, 5, 167; heterogeneity, 21–22, 130; and subject
formation, 103

Desire, 5; and colonialism, 14; as
discursively produced, 14, 29; as
an embedded process, 4–5, 10, 79;
epistemology of, 24, 27; fluid, 23;
according to Hegel, 167n15; heterogeneous, 34, 130; and history, 124, 161;
incomplete, 154; inconsistent, 8, 13,
93; and interiority, 32; and Islamic
activist women, 4, 9,13, 16–17, 19,

50, 59, 77, 82, 93–95, 97, 98, 118, 155;
according to Lacan, 167n15; liberal/
non liberal, 10–11, 104; postcolonial,
13, 16, 102; as a productive process,
3, 73; as rhizomatic, 5, 78, 102; and
secularism, and religion, 6, 8–9, 17,
25, 79, 157, 162; self-fashioning desire,
92, 149; Suad, Joseph, on, 12, 157; and
subjectivity, 12; by *tagdid al-niyya*,
110–111, 117, 157, 167

Desiring subjects, 12–13, 102–104,
124; activist women of al-Hilal, 6;
ethnographers as, 23; and discourse.
18; modern, 12, 17, 148; resistant, 13;
selves as, 167

Development: embedded modern,
17, 39, 128, 130, 133; Islamic, 129;
sustainable, 16, 39, 129, 149; in village
of Mehmeit, 128, 134–136, 146, 150;
women's Islamic, 17, 93, 135, 149, 154;
as worship, 130

Dichotomy: and housework, 88;
Islamic and secular, 47, 154; modernity and tradition, 75); religious
and secular subjects, 79. *See also*
Binary

din, 38, 163; *Al-din lil lah wa'l wattan lil
gami'*, 92; vs. *dini*, 170; *din wa dawla*,
125; *dunya* and, 116; *durus din*, 81

Discipline, 169; and colonialism, 56,
125; and confession, the ritual of,
40; disciplined citizens, 60, 93, 124;
modern techniques of, 9, 56, 99, 131;
and mothering, 113, 155; and production, 146; and punctuality, 83, 99, 132,
149; religious discipline, 10; self-, 110,
111; and the state, 16

Domestic sphere, 74, 99, 131, 101;
reform of, 155; as regulatory space,
15, 131, 156

dunya, 116, 163, 170n18

Durkheim, Emile, 33–34, 35, 50

Inculcation of piety and religious discipline, 10; desire in, 5; and liberal modern values, 130; resistance to, 13; in subjectivity, 9

infitah (an "open door" policy), 59, 163

Interiority of religious experience, 32, 40, 10; and individuality, 6; as inseparable from exteriority in subject making processes, 32; in James, William, 31; in rituals of confession, 40

Islam, 11, 52, 63; air-conditioned, 55; militant, 71, 166, 168; Islamist groups, 7, 9, 11, 43, 52, 67–68, 70, 78, 121, 125, 152, 156; Islamist women, 70, 160, 168, 170; as a state, 53, 63, 125; women's Islamic activism, 67, 74, 77, 87, 98, 106, 150, 153. *See also* Islam, "enlightened"

Islam, "enlightened," 56, 171; and anti-imperialism, 60, 67; and authenticity, 63, 65; and embedded discourses, 56, 75; Islamism, 6, 8, 23, 50, 55; Islam-ization, 4, 9, 10, 11, 44, 52, 54, 59, 122, 73; resurgence, 59; Salafi Islam, 60, 97, 164, 169, 171; and the state, 53

Islamic feminism, 7, 67, 153, 165, 166

Islamic movements: and subjectivity 8, 162; and desire, 50, 52–59, 154, 157, 160

Islamic Salvation Front (FIS), 159

Islamic social reform: al-Ghazali, Abdel Hamid, on social development, 68; sustainable development, 6, 7, 39, 68, 123, 129, 133. *See also* Development

Islamic Tendency Movements (MTI), 160

James, William 31, 34

Joseph, Suad: on desire and relational pedagogies, 12, 21; on feminist reflexivity, 21

Khaled, Amr, 54, 160

khimar, 22, 23, 151, 163

Kipnis, Andrew: analysis of Falun Gong, 47

kuttab, 60

Liberal(s), 10, 52, 56; in Egypt, 56, 59, 157, 163; inculcated in citizens, 13, 51, 155; Islamic, 121, 158; liberal and nonliberal agency, 9, 104; liberalism, 167; liberal models of development, 12, 17, 113, 128; liberal notion of self-hood, 12, 78; liberatory subjectivity, 125; nonliberal, 9, 10, 11, 102; secular values, 14, 83, 95, 99, 104, 130, 131, 133, 149

Literacy, 7, 70, 73, 80, 132, 133; classes, 70, 80, 140, 135, 147; illiteracy, 73, 97; literacy village center, 123

MacIntyre, Alasdair, 167

Magic, mystical-magical, 32, 34, 35, 37, 38

Mahmood, Saba, critique of notions of liberal agency, 11–12

Malinowski, Bronislaw, on religion and reason among the Trobrianders, 37–38

Mecca pilgrimage, 170; and the term *hagga,* 72; and veiling, 89, 163, 84

Mediated subjectivity, 132, 172

Mehmeit: village, 138; project, 128–133, 146–148. *See also* Village of Mehmeit

Middle class, 69, 22; and al-Hilal, 82, 83, 86, 118, 119; in Egyptian society, 82, 86; and militant groups, 71

Ministry of Religious Endowments, 84, 109

Mitchell, Tim: analysis of the state, 16; on projects of modernization, 57, 60, 62

mo'amalat, 84, 125

Modernity, 13, 19, 27, 32, 49, 131, 157, 158, 166; and activist women, 88, 125; "advanced modernity," 48; and ethics,

43; as a form of imperialism, 60; imbricated with Islamic principles, 91, 98, 100, 148, 155; Islam binary, 4, 23, 45, 52, 43, 67; religious binary, 9, 28, 44, 104, 154; and subjectivity, 11, 15, 18, 79; vs. tradition, 31, 44, 51, 75, 166; women as vehicles of modernity, 62

Modernization, 100, 166; and British colonialism, 63; in Egypt, 60, 100, 121; effects on women, 62, 74, 155, 168; in the family, 62; and Islamic groups, 160; and religion, 15, 61, 158; and religion in state discourse, 51, 95, and subject production, 7, 10, 13, 79, 80, 93, 125; and women's Islamic activism, 16, 38, 78, 101, 130; and modesty, 10, 11; and veiling, 10

MOSA, Ministry of Social Affairs, 20

Musa, Nabawiyya, 64

Muslim Brotherhood, 52; Abul Fadl, Amany, 151; al-Banna, Hassan, founder, 67; al-Ghazali, Zeinab, 68–69; and Islamization, 53; and Nasser, Gamal Abdel, 68; opposition to the state, 57, 97; popularity, 52, 130; scholar's views on FGM, 152; social activism, 67; on social development, 129; views on women, 58, 68

Muslim Women's Association, 67

Narratives of conversion, 88, 92; as an illusion of wholeness, 93; as modern discourse, 18–19, 91

nashid, 55, 163

Nasif, Malak Hefni, 64–66

Nationalism: after 1967 war, 69; Arab, 69, 71; and desire, 4; Egyptian, 59, 71; "religious nationalism," 44–45, 74; and subjectivity; 11, 13; and westernization, 65; and women activists, 94; and women's movements, 66, 74, 46

Nongovernmental organizations (NGOs), 151; and FGM, 152

Ottoman period, 61; harem life, 61; upper class, 62

Personhood; Islamic, construction of, 17, 19, 78, 117; refashioning, 149; and Western domination, 14. *See also* Selfhood

Piety movement, 10

Polygamy, 63

Postcolonial, 13, 17; and cultural hybrids, 21, 104; desire and sub-jectivity, 5, 8, 10, 13, 16, 19, 59, 124; education, 56; and Islam, 15; and liberal secular projects, 157; nation-state, 17, 56

Postmodern subjectivity, 102–103. *See also* Subjectivity

Poverty alleviation, Islamic projects of, 7, 71, 86, 128, 129, 133, 134, 148

Power, 59; and desire, 16; and discursive processes, 14, 40, 41, 50, 79; disciplinary power, 16; and the disempowerment of women, 156; empowerment of women, 2, 7, 8, 12, 20; and the ethnographic process, 20–21; in the history of religion, 29, 41; and subject production, 8, 12; and social development, 149; Western, and imperialism, 14, 42, 159

Prayer, 80, 82, 84, 85, 91, 120, 128, 147, 172n4; funerary, 107

Preachers, 2, 54, 84, 109, 160, 163, 170n4. See also *da'iyat*

Private Voluntary Organization (P.V.O), 1, 7, 20, 80, 160

Progress, 32, 100, 131; and religion, 11, 28, 31, 35, 42, 43, 63, 107; and women, 58, 64

Prophet Muhammad, 55, 94, 114, 164, 168n17; *hadith* 106, 108, 111, 171n16; *al-sira-al-Nabawiyya,* 108; *sunnah,* 168n16

Qazim, Safinaz, 70

Qur'an, 63, 84, 96, 106, 111, 117, 132, 163, 164, 168n17, 170n8, 172n4; and funerals, 107; interpretation, 11; Qur'anic recital, 108, 132, 139, 143, 147, 165n2; Qur'anic studies, 108, 109, 169n18; and women, 61

Rabinah, 95, 112, 113, 164

Raouf, Heba, 1

Rationality and emotions, 24, 42; and ethics, 43, and Islam, 173; and non literate societies, 37, 38; and progress, 35; and religion, 27, 35, 36, 50; liberal secular, 14, 157, 166

Religion(s), 47, 71; as an analytical category, 27, 28, 29, 30, 31, 32, 33, 34, 35, 36, 40, 41, 44, 49, 162; to Islamic activist women, 13, 38, 78, 89, 93, 95, 96, 101, 102, 109, 110, 112, 114, 116, 121, 123, 124, 134, 170, 171; knowledge of, 120; and modernity, 9, 28, 42, 43, 46, 49, 57, 74, 104, 158, 160; and rationality, 35, 36, 168n1; religious lessons, 140; religious nationalism, 44–45, 46, 74; religious patchworks, 48; "religious subjectivity," 33, 35, 49; and secularism; 4, 5, 8, 9, 12, 15, 25, 38, 40, 44, 46, 48, 50, 51, 58, 60, 63, 78, 79, 92, 99, 122, 124, 125, 154, 155, 156, 159, 161, 166n11. See also *din*

Resistance, 10, 42, 65

Rhizome, 5, 102, 103; rhizomatic desire, 5

Rotary Inner Wheel, 93, 122; as distinct from Islamic organizations, 93–94, 123

Sadat, Anwar, 68; assassination of, 70–71, 168; *infitah* policies, 71, 169

Said, Edward: on culture, 28; and Orientalism, 14, 27

Schooling, 15–16, 22, 60; boy's, 62; girl's, 66. *See also* Education

Science, 28, 29, 38, 48, 147, 170; and religion, 29, 31, 35, 37, 38, 39, 40, 47, 50, 110, 159

Secularism, 48, 66, 74, 78, 79, 159, 163; Arabic term for, 170; and modernity, 6, 15, 46. *See also,* Religion(s), and secularism

Seif al-Dawla, Aida, 151–153

Self, 12; autonomous, 103; bounded, 91, 92; Cartesian view of, 102; connective self, 21; and desire, 157; liberal notions of, 12; and modern narratives, 18, 91; modern selfhood, 6, 14; Muslim, 18, 56, 78, 93, 113, 118; vs. the notion of the subject, 171; self-construction, 15, 18, 78, 100, 115; self-fashioning, 5, 11, 12, 17, 19, 78, 84, 88, 92, 102, 131, 149; selfhood, 19; self-image, 90; self-reflexivity, 19, 21; pious, 6, 92, 158; porous, 21. *See also* Discipline, self-

Shafik, Doria, 69

Sha'rawi, Hoda, 65–66, 70

Shari'a, Shari'a law, 78, 80, 129, 164, 168, 170, 173; secularization of, 15, 57, 58; training in, 109, 119; and women, 20

Subjectivity, 8, 14, 36, 49, 98; and desire, 12, 32, 39, 59; discursive, 5, 79, 157; heterogenous, x, 4, 17, 25, 34, 154; mediated, 132, 172n1; Muslim subjectivities, 50; "religious subjectivity," 24, 27, 28, 51, 99; religious/secular, 157; subject-making processes, 5, 9, 13; subject production, 25, 131, 133,157; Sufism, 90, 117, 171n12; unitary subject, 4

tajdid al niyya, 93, 95, 110, 111, 171n3

Teymour, Aisha, 61

Tunisia, 158, 160

Turkey, 126, 158

Tylor, Edward, 31, 35, 37, 50

'ulama, 60, 61, 62, 64, 164

Veiling practices. See *hijab*

Village of Mehmeit, 138, 146; al-Hilal social reform project, 133–150; contractual relationship, 132, 172n1; village homes, 135, 136, 140–142, 145; village women, 128, 135, 137, 144, 146, 148, 149; vocational training, micro loans, 132–133

Weber, Max, 34

Westernization, 62, 63, 65, 66–67

Women's Feminist Movement, Egypt, 7, 58, 64–68, 153–154

Women's Islamic activism, 130

Yunis, Mona, 90–91

About the Author

SHERINE HAFEZ is Assistant Professor in the Department of Women's Studies at the University of California, Riverside. She is the author of *The Terms of Empowerment: Islamic Women Activists in Egypt*.

EDITORIAL V *Verbum*

Títulos publicados:

PEDRO AULLÓN DE HARO:
La obra poética de Gil de Biedma (ensayo)

JOSÉ LEZAMA LIMA:
La Habana (ensayos)

JOSÉ TRIANA:
Teatro: Medea en el espejo, La noche de los asesinos y Palabras comunes

JEAN PAUL RICHTER:
Introducción a la Estética (ensayo)

DARIE NOVACEANU:
Estado del tiempo (poemas)

EDUARDO MORA-ANDA:
Palabras Personales (poemas)

FILOTEO SAMANIEGO:
Sobre sismos y otros miedos (novela)

RENÁN FLORES JARAMILLO:
El oscuro oleaje de los días (novela)

PEDRO SHIMOSE:
América vista por los europeos (antología)